MALACHI O'DOHERTY was born in Muff, County Donegal, in 1951 and grew up in west Belfast. He has made his living mostly as a freelance journalist and broadcaster, appearing on the BBC's *Sunday Sequence* and *Talkback* programmes, and writing regularly for the *Belfast Telegraph*. Now Writer in Residence at Queen's University Belfast, he is the author of a number of books including *I Was a Teenage Catholic* (2003), *The Telling Year* (2007) and *Under His Roof* (2009), a series of vignettes about his father.

D0522952

ON MY OWN TWO WHEELS

BACK IN THE SADDLE AT 60

MALACHI O'DOHERTY

BLACKSTAFF PRESS
BELFAST

With thanks to Bike Dock for practical
support and advice.

First published in 2012 by
Blackstaff Press
4c Heron Wharf
Sydenham Business Park
Belfast BT3 9LE
with the assistance of
The Arts Council of Northern Ireland

arts
council
of Northern Ireland

Typeset by CJWT Solutions, St Helens, England

Printed in Great Britain by the MPG Books Group

A CIP catalogue record for this book is available from the British Library

ISBN 978 0 85640 889 2

www.blackstaffpress.com

www.blackstaffpress.com/ebooks

For Maureen

only moving
does it have a soul
and fallen there
it isn't
a translucent insect
humming
through summer
but
a cold
skeleton
that will return to
life
only
when it's needed,
when it's light,
that is,
with
the
resurrection
of each day.

Pablo Neruda, *Ode to Bicycles*

Contents

1 Oh sugar!

It started with a pinprick and a glass of Lucozade, or something similarly gloopy and sweet. I had asked my doctor to screen me for diabetes. I was in a risk category – I was fat and I had had stomach troubles and I knew I wasn't as fit as I should be. Now I was at the doctor's surgery, in the hands of a nurse with plastic gloves on, a needle that didn't look too threatening and a little electronic monitor.

The first reading of my blood sugar level was 8.3. I had been fasting from the night before.

'Is that high?'

'Well, we have to send a sample away for a proper reading. Drink this.'

She handed me a glass of the rich sugary – warm! – liquid and encouraged me to drink it down. It slithered into me.

'Now wait in the reception area for two hours and we'll test you again.' She had the manner of someone acting on legal advice and clearly wasn't going to say anything that might either increase or assuage my anxieties. I have seen policemen in the witness stand who were garrulous by comparison.

Two hours is a long time in a waiting area, watching other people come and go. A reporter I know came in and sat beside me for a minute to say hello. I discovered that the common exchanges we make with each other don't apply when you think the other person might be ill and you don't want to probe. You don't say, 'Hi, are you well?' You say, 'I hope things are fine with you; have a good day.'

The sugary drink had made me giddy, but that soon settled and my mind began to play over what had brought me to this test. One thing was age. I was approaching my sixtieth birthday and I wasn't happy about that at all. As the birthday approached, my wife Maureen hinted at the idea of a party and I told her I could see nothing at all to celebrate about getting older and inching closer to decrepitude and death. I had been similarly morose on my fiftieth. Then, Maureen had brought me breakfast on a tray with a card and a present and said, 'Happy birthday.' I said, 'What's there to be happy about? – a birthday just marks time passing and running out.'

But my sixtieth was worse. Many of the people I had looked up to and learnt from had finished their life's work at sixty or before. At fifty I had wondered what sixty would be like and I sat in a meeting for an arts-type committee with others, talking about age – because I'd told them it was my birthday – and about the meaning of different periods in life. One of the company was a man of sixty and to me he looked slack and unfocused, amiable and harmless. The thought that that was coming to me was just demoralising. It didn't occur to me that he might have been slack and unfocused at twenty as well.

Friends tried to reason with me: 'What's the point in being miserable about being sixty when you can't change it?' I replied, 'So you're only allowed to be unhappy about things you can change? Life is limited; there isn't enough of it. That's awful.'

The number of years available to me now seemed too easy to encompass in my imagination. In twenty years I would be eighty. You don't see a lot of fat eighty-year-olds out on the street. I could cast my mind back easily to when I was forty, facing a similar need to reassess myself, and it seemed just a few months back. For it's worse than time just running out like sands through an hourglass; time accelerates as you grow older. The decade between being twenty and thirty is about twice as long as the one between forty and fifty. Check it yourself.

I was resolved to live into my nineties anyway, though if I am honest I would really like another fifty or sixty years beyond that; by that stage I am sure I will have got the hang of the things that matter.

Another reason for my visit to the nurse was that I knew I wasn't fit. I have a twin brother Roger. We are so alike that people could not tell the difference between us when we were growing up. The previous summer we had together walked up Knocklayde, the mountain that looms over Ballycastle in County Antrim. That was fun, though we took a ridiculously circuitous route that ended in a steep climb. He made it to the top and I had to give up. Now, that shouldn't happen with twins. As children, our classmates would sometimes pit us against each other in arm-wrestling matches that were usually deadlocked. Now two stone lighter, and clearly fitter, he was climbing mountains that defeated me.

The two hours passed and the nurse with the plastic gloves was pricking me again.

'What is it this time?' Again, she didn't want to say. I didn't know then that I could have bought one of those testers for under a tenner and found out the figure for myself. I know a lot more about diabetes now.

'It's 11.8,' she finally told me.

Still, it was only numbers.

'Does that mean I am diabetic?'

'It's in that area.'

'Well, what would be a worrying figure?'

'If it was over twenty we probably wouldn't let you go home.'

The result only confirmed what I'd already suspected. Even before the test I had started to make changes. I had been walking more; even bought myself a pair of MBTs. Those are the big clumpy shoes that are brilliantly branded as making you effectively barefoot – Barefoot Technology – though they are as thick as bricks. They are the sort of thing that would have been sold twenty years ago as 'approved by doctors' and nobody would have bought them. The M stands for Masai; you can be a Masai warrior with bricks on your feet. Pure marketing genius!

This was shaping up to be one of those cusp-of-decade moments in my life when I resolved to make big changes. Securing a stable and sane relationship had been one of my fortieth birthday resolutions. I had been married to Maureen for most of the period since. In the comfort of our marriage I had filled out nicely and slowed down. I hadn't been up enough mountains and I hadn't been out on my bicycle for over a decade. Now, when I sat at the table for dinner I had a belly that seemed to sit on my lap like an importunate child asking for ice cream or another glass of wine. I had just accepted that gradual fattening was a normal part of ageing and that I was turning into a tubby man who wasn't meant to ride a bike.

And I didn't look very fat except when I was naked and the one person who shared that body did not complain. I learnt to dress to accommodate the big blunt belly in front of me. I wore braces rather than a belt. A lot of fat men go on wearing tight trousers but belt them low, so the large paunch can sit out over the waistband and buckle. These men kid themselves that they are still thirty-six inches around the waist, but they don't even have a waist and have taken to wearing their trousers round their hips. I wore waistcoats that smoothed the line of the paunch from the chest to the lower abdomen, disguising its alarming thrust forward and giving an impression of affable and prosperous rotundity. I looked my worst in trim shirts and tight jumpers. People would then say, 'You're filling out a bit, aren't you?' They hadn't noticed that I had been fat for years.

With being fat came the embarrassing discomforts of

flatulence and urgency and cramp. I had been going to the doctor complaining of mysterious pains in my side. Could it be gallstones? My liver? It never seemed to be anything in particular – because it was congestion. And there was an answer: eat less, exercise more, enjoy your nimble body and live longer. Irritable bowel, stomach cramps, reflux, heart scares and a hernia – I had so many problems that seemed to trace back to nothing in particular, I was beginning to think I was a hypochondriac. I wasn't. I was a fat man with a body that gave him no peace.

And I snored. All that added bulk, resting on my diaphragm, and the fat filling out my neck and cheeks, combined with the thickening of my larynx and nasal passages to provide low thunder in the bedroom. The solution was the same as that for every other problem: eat less, walk more, get back on the bike. Instead I went to a dentist called Andrew. Andrew, though a trim man, had a snoring problem himself and had developed a client base of other noisy sleepers. He fitted me with a little gumshield that drew my lower jaw forward, widening the space for breath behind it. This device clamped on to the upper row of teeth. A projection from the front of it back towards the tongue caught the lower teeth and held them out. It took me a little time to get used to this and I went back to Andrew to have irritating edges refined. But it was a wonder. It worked and I learned to sleep in perfect comfort with it in. I even slept more deeply now that my own snoring was not waking me up. I would have to take the shield out if we were getting affectionate before going to sleep and remember to put it back in afterwards, but this was good for me and good for her. Maureen was delighted – she joked that she wanted to send Andrew flowers. But I only needed the thing because I was fat. I could have sorted that problem out myself but no one really expects you to.

I grew up in a culture which absolved me of carelessness with my body, that assessed my manliness by my demeanour as I smoked and drank. There was a thread of fatalism in all our thinking. When I was young and smoked and people said it would kill me, I knew the answer I had heard from others: 'Sure you could get run over by a bus in the morning.'

For a time it seemed almost as if we had a revolutionary responsibility to defy the paternalism that cautioned you to live a healthy life. On one side of the line were prissy and clean, compliant and religious stooges who had sold out on the prospects of a fun life; on the other were the defiant individuals – all of us in the standard blue denim uniform of our kind – smoking and drinking and having sex outside marriage, which was in the same category of anarchic defiance when I was twenty. We used to pass round the 'cancer sticks' and laugh off the solicitousness of a nanny state as if the right to poison yourself was a noble one worth defending through sarcasm and contempt – it felt like rugged individualism.

Indeed, when you woke up in the morning with a hangover and coughing you felt that life was a great physical challenge and that you were bearing up well if you could clear the gunk and light another fag. In my own fantasies this seemed to get bound up with images of ardent struggle, placated a myth that you were doing something, up against the odds, and even more so if you were in a cold flat paid for through the dole. At a certain age smoking and drinking can look manly because the people who do it have the washed-out look of cowboys who have come thousands of miles on the back of a horse.

One of the most amazing things about the modern city is that you can draw a map of it marking the places where people are most likely to adhere still to habits that will shorten their lives. This suggests that there is little more to preserving your health and longevity than becoming middle class. In the city that I live in, Belfast, the average life span on one road can be fourteen years longer than that on another road just a few miles away. You can predict how long people will live by how much their house is worth. But for individuals, health and wellbeing are not an inheritance. Many of us started out in a toxic culture and learnt a better way to live.

A week after my visit to the nurse, I had an appointment with my doctor. His advice was simple and straightforward: If you could lose a stone you'd hardly know yourself.' Weight loss has better medical outcomes than heart bypass surgery. The doctor prodded my feet with a plastic rod the size of a toothpick to check that I retained sensation in them. He was checking whether the diabetes had so reduced my blood circulation that I was in danger of stepping on a nail or piece of glass and not feeling it – diabetics sometimes only find the cuts after they have become infected. This was the strangest medical test I had ever had, like a search for a tickle. I was fine, but the doctor warned me that I should never again walk round the house in my bare feet. Then, he listened to my heart. He discussed the relative merits and dangers of taking aspirin every day and sent me away with a sheaf of pages to read about how it was actually okay to have the odd ice cream because you have to enjoy life, don't you? The good old National Health, breaking the news gently and offering you a get-out clause.

Of course, nobody expects you to be able to reform. I know obese people who have horrendous difficulty losing weight and keeping it off. My sister Brid was occasionally enormous but her weight would fluctuate horrendously, in keeping with her volatile emotional character. I wasn't that type of fatty. I was just an ordinary thinnish sort of bloke who had let himself go. My gamble was that if I could get my weight down to what it had been twenty years earlier it would stay there, or at worst, it would creep back up only as insidiously as before, buying me some time. There is now a campaign against dieting that insists people should be told it doesn't work. But I know a lot of people who have had the willpower to give up smoking so why shouldn't as many people be able to control their weight? Others, like my mother, for instance, simply couldn't and the fags killed her, but the plain evidence of life in the workplace now is that most people aren't puffing away like they used to.

For me, losing weight wasn't nearly as hard as getting off cigarettes. I have also suffered withdrawal from relationships that didn't work and that was worse – nights of anguished struggle against the impulse to phone. The chief danger for me was that I would drop my guard and think, 'One fag / one pavlova / one more attempt to grovel on my knees before her, and tomorrow I'll be sensible again.' I had cracked the fags by personifying the addiction in my mind as a malicious seducer who would destroy me with a tease. Temptation had to be treated with contempt, and abruptly. When Satan, masquerading as my own thoughts, said things like, 'One more spud is hardly going to hurt you,' I had to cast him from me, back into the fiery pit. I needed my inner voice to be a disciplinarian, a real tub-thumper, fine-tuned to condemn sugar.

The diabetes that I have does not require medication, just sensible diet. That doesn't mean that you should go on a diet, if dieting means taking a temporary break from eating as you like: I have a woman friend who, when on a diet, said she longed for it to end so that she could enjoy banoffee pie again. I was out to change my way of eating for all time. I would give up sugary stodge, I hoped, with the same finality with which I had given up cigarettes.

So I was going to have to be my own boot camp sergeant. The doctor wasn't going to bully me, probably because he had discovered with others before me that it doesn't work; that sugar, toxic in the doses we are at ease with, usually wins in the end. The core advice on diet was to lose weight gradually, not to rush at it, not to starve myself, just to cut down and aim to lose about two pounds a week. I was twelve stone five most times I weighed myself. This varied from day to day and morning to evening. We don't have a static weight. Once you start monitoring yourself you can find two or three pounds of difference between morning and evening. A glass of water weighs nearly a pound. Which is your true weight: you with or without the water? Athletes trying to make their proper weight at the Commonwealth Games in India would lose three pounds by skipping under the hot sun and still, apparently, be in a fit condition to compete.

I could remember being just eight stone as a teenager and I have no idea what I was in between because I never had the habit of checking. My body mass index calculations showed that I was not underweight when I was eight stone though I look scrawny in the old photographs. I am a small man, but I could barely conceive of myself as so light now. The range the calculations allowed me said I also would not be overweight at ten stone. The index allowed me a latitude of nearly thirty-seven pounds within which I would be a healthy weight. But it was June when I got my diagnosis and I set a target of getting down to ten stone by Christmas. That would take me just to the very top of that allowable band and it would allow for an even more gradual decline than two pounds a week.

I gave up all sweets and desserts, and would rise from most meals feeling peckish still, but soon discovered that this feeling passed after about ten minutes, especially if I drank a glass of water. The weight went down in stepped stages. It would drop half a stone over a few weeks and then doggedly refuse to drop further for a month, then resume the decline, as if having confirmed that I was serious in my intention. Where I might have finished most of a bottle of wine with my dinner I cut it out most nights and kept to one glass at most. I stopped snacking on biscuits and buying bars of chocolate on my walks. At first this was hard because I love food. I can think of nothing more appealing than a new potato, smooth as marble after the fine papery skin has been peeled off, dripping with golden butter, perhaps with a whole smoked cod or haddock, maybe with a poached egg on top and a pint of stout to help wash it down. I am not ascetic by nature. I had enjoyed getting fat, had thought it almost fair penance for the pleasure food and drink gave me – until my health was in danger. Then I reasoned myself out of gluttony, partly by noticing that the greatest satisfaction from any feast is in the first few bites, that a single chocolate savoured and allowed to melt on the tongue brings all the joy of a full dessert.

According to my body mass index I was obese at the start of the diet. By Christmas I was not even overweight. I had touched ten stone and still hovered just over it by a couple of pounds a year later, having neither bounced back up nor plunged into skeletal self-effacement. And I felt different in several ways. Friends could see the change most markedly on my face. They didn't know that when I took my shirt off I still had a tubby wee tummy sagging like a bag in front of me, even if it was a lot smaller now than the hulk of fat that had squatted there before. I hadn't expected my hands to change but my fingers thinned and just holding familiar things or typing would remind me that I had a new body. I stopped using the anti-snoring device because I didn't need it any more. My whole body was lighter, trimmer and fitter. I didn't get out of breath walking or going upstairs. Sometimes I would lift a bale of peat briquettes to remind myself how much extra weight I had been carrying everywhere I went, all day every day, just a few months before. And, knowing that readers will not want a detailed account of the functioning of my alimentary canal, I can at least say it was happy to have so much less work to do and did it better.

People commented on my weight loss everywhere I went. Friends didn't like it – they worried about me and were afraid that I was becoming obsessive. Some expressed alarm, asked me if I was ill. Some complimented me. Some just stared, trying to work out what was different and then asked, 'Have you lost weight?' You would think that body size, health and diets are private matters that acquaintances and colleagues would not enquire into, but few people seem inclined to constrain their curiosity and wonder when they notice that you are lighter or heavier than you previously have been. I was enjoying my food and still going to nice restaurants – if eating smaller portions – yet there is such anxiety about the prospect of dieting turning into anorexia, becoming compulsive or being governed by delusions, that Maureen and others would constantly urge me to stop and not lose more.

Some asked me for advice: 'What diet did you use?' I told them I used the 'smaller portions diet'. I remember one day in my fatness sitting on a high stool in a television studio, adjusting my position according to the monitor, and wondering how to conceal a stomach that sat in my lap like a parcel. I couldn't hold it in if I was to speak to the camera. I joked about the problem with the studio manager, thinking he might have a practical suggestion. He said, 'I am the same and I asked a doctor friend. He says there is no mystery: weight gain is caused by putting food in your mouth and swallowing it.' The joke is on those who affect to be bewildered.

But my fatness had crept up on me slowly and I learnt quickly that what worked for me in getting rid of it makes little sense to others. A woman friend asked me for advice on how to lose weight. I said: 'Learn to think of peckishness as natural and good for you. Eat what you need and enjoy it, then stop and resist the temptation to pile more in until you feel full. Drink water instead. If you're not really hungry that peckishness passes. You know how it is sometimes in a restaurant? You call for an extra portion of chips because you love them but there's a delay and when they finally arrive you don't feel like eating them anymore. The peckishness has passed. Well, love peckishness and trust it to go away.' She said, 'I don't know what you're talking about. My problem is not that I feel peckish but that I feel ravenous. Leave the last spud in the pot because you don't need it? I do need it.'

So it makes little sense sometimes to frame the argument for self-improvement and healthy living as a failure of individual people to manage their appetites. The advice is around us all the time to cut down on drinking and smoking, to eat better and to be healthier and happier. And most of the time we don't take it.

2 My father's son

Some men at sixty buy themselves a sports car and start chasing women much younger than themselves. I was suffering from exactly the same condition; I wanted to be the man I had been at thirty. I didn't have the money for the car and I hoped I had more sense than to take a young lover, even if they were that easy to come by.

When I turned sixty, after I'd got my weight down, I bought myself a nice little trim leather jacket. I could not have worn anything like it in the past twenty years without betraying a paunch. Now I looked slimmer in it than I actually was. People who hadn't noticed my weight loss could see it more clearly. I looked a bit more like James Dean and a bit less like Danny DeVito; or, at least, I had moved along the spectrum between them. Change your clothes and you're a different person. I should have known that.

But could I not actually have back some of the life that I had then? Other men might recover a sense of being young by living out the playboy years they feel they missed. The years that called me back were my thirties when I cycled all over the country and developed a hard and wiry wee body without even feeling that I was working at it. I could cycle a hundred miles in a day. The last time I had gone out on my bike I had felt my knees pressing up into my big stomach and discovered that I was simply no longer shaped for a bicycle. But that had changed, hadn't it? I was a man with a new body. I could wear trim leather jackets. Could I still ride a bike? Could I ride for hours into the countryside, eat my sandwiches under a tree and be a free spirit?

I think I am genetically disposed to cycling. Nature has not shaped me to race but it has instilled the love of bicycles in me. What's the evidence here for nature rather than nurture being the influence? Well, there have been bikers in every generation of my family that I know about. I have nephews whose Facebook profiles depict them in their coloured club shirts cornering on mountain roads.

And this must have come down to them, at least in part, from my father – who had raced, but did nothing to encourage me to cycle at all. Heredity is the only explanation for a quivering lust for biking that has been with me since I was a child. Unless the denial of my need for a bike raised it to a passion in me, and the person to blame for that is the father who never bought me one. Well, perhaps that's it. The bicycle is a forbidden joy indulged more eagerly for the feeling that it represents freedom from the old rules. So it symbolises transgression for me but with fewer complications than other sins might bring.

I was never going to be an athlete or a racer like my father was. For a start, I am small. After a physically exuberant early childhood in which I ran and jumped and wrestled like a puppy, I discovered that I could not compete with other boys. The race was indeed with the swift, and I was not one of them. So I grew up with the expectation that I would never do anything marvellous with my body. I never really aspired to being fit nor expected to be. As a small man I was a low achiever in sports. That fact defined me. School sports day was always an embarrassment because every other boy could run faster and jump further than I could. The one time I was a hero on the pitch was when I was asked to make up a team to its minimum allowable strength, so that a game could go ahead that would otherwise have been cancelled. My instructions were to run away from the ball if it came anywhere near me. With that tactic, I saved the day, and though I wasn't carried off on shoulders, I was allowed to change and dry out in front of a heater in the principal's office.

I wasn't competitive but I was light and nimble and enjoyed physical play. I often went walking in the Belfast Hills on Sunday afternoons, scrambling through hedges, jumping ditches, braving fierce fences. But I thought of myself as a physical inadequate. I was always last picked for a team.

I weighed eight stone in my teens. In my twenties I wore trousers with a thirty-inch waist and this went up to thirty-two inches a few years later. I had no interest in sports but I was reasonably healthy and mobile. In the mid-1970s and at the age of twenty-four, I went to India and took up the discipline of yoga under a Hindu monk called Swami Paramananda Saraswati. This routine included a set of fifteen asanas or postures, which I repeated every morning and night. I was not a good yogi. A westerner uses the legs differently from an Indian. We don't sit on the floor, legs folded, so we lose the suppleness we had as children. We don't relax by squatting with the bum resting on the back of the heels as Indians do. So I was never going to be more than moderately accomplished. Still, I did headstands and various bending poses and did loosen up. My favourite pose was the Ardamatsayendra asana in which I twisted my spine and cracked vertebrae in sequence, the way I would crack my knuckles.

And eventually I accomplished a very tight lotus posture, with each foot resting upturned on the opposite thigh. I couldn't hold it for long but I could incorporate it into another asana called the Peacock. In this I would get into the lotus posture, and lift myself up on to my hands with my elbows pressed into my stomach. I would hold myself there for maybe a minute. I doubt it did me much good but it was a party piece in later years.

It was after my time in India that I worked for a couple of years in Libya teaching English for a Swiss company training the Air Defence Forces. Having to maintain a confident front before a gang of working men and teach unhappy young conscripts was a sharp contrast with floating along the banks of the Ganges in a dreamy haze. It was a toughening up that I needed after years of introspective reflection on mysticism and poetry. I got recruited into the job while living in Geneva with my girlfriend, Celine.

In Libya I kept fit by swimming in the pool – I learnt to swim when I was there – and working out in a gym that the company had provided for us. At first I would just lay out a mat and do my asanas then skip rope for a while. But I didn't get the emotional release from the stress of the job until I discovered the punchball. Then I would unleash pent up aggression by thumping it until I was breathless and spent. That strategy failed me one day when my aggression, instead of using itself up in violence against the ball, just grew stronger and stronger until I was in a fury. It was time to leave Libya.

I've also done a little hill walking and weights training. The hill walking was a natural extension of the childhood pleasure of rambling over Black Mountain and Divis, where I had had the added thrill of trespassing on private land and quarries. Hill walking was another way of doing the things I most enjoyed, sleeping in a tent under the stars, waking in the morning in the open air, washing in a river, wandering over fields and hills away from everybody, where you can shout your thoughts and notions, stand naked in the wind.

Biking, as physical exertion, was superior to all other kinds for it doubled as a form of transport. Boxing a punch ball provided no such return.

I don't think that the hill walking or the cycling were motivated by the desire to be physically fitter and I wonder if the desire to be fit, in itself, is not a bit questionable. If we lived the natural lives our evolution had prepared us for we would be fit anyway. To concede the need to get fit is to acknowledge that your life is unnatural. Why not just go the whole hog and fix your life then? When I devoted my efforts to fitness, in itself, I was bored. Nature didn't prime me to lift weights in repetitive cycles for the sole purpose of building muscle. Nature designed the body so that it would get stronger when that strength was to be deployed for the work it had to do.

Okay, my usual work of writing on a computer keyboard doesn't do much for your thighs. Going to a gym is a form of confession; it declares that your life is not suited to your body, and worse, you can't think of any more productive or enjoyable way to lose weight and build muscle, to restore yourself to your natural state, than by repetitive action. Well, that may be great for some people. The pleasure at the end is in the feeling of physical wellbeing and enjoying the sight of the body in the mirror. As for me, I'd usually rather go out on the bike. When I go wandering in the hills or cycling along the coast I am not grasping control of my life but surrendering it. I am conceding that I am amenable to unpredictable things happening to me.

The da, on the other hand, was a racer.

I have a photograph of him from a Derry newspaper in the 1930s. The book in which it is reproduced gives no date or caption but he is recognisable there even though he is wholly unlike the man I knew. The photographer had gathered twenty men and boys of the club to meet at the point they raced from on the road to Limavady on a wet summer evening. None of them are wearing cycling gear that would be familiar as such now, though one or two of the older men have knickerbockers, to avoid trouser legs flapping into the crank wheel and getting snagged on the chain. They stand with their various bicycles, most of them racing bikes with drop handlebars of the kind that are still popular, though they are called road bikes now. Some of the bikes have straight handlebars and broad tyres more suited to city streets than racing. A working man in those days would only have had one bike and might have had to compromise.

My father is posed on a sleek racer but – paradoxically – is wearing a jacket and tie. His hair is gelled and brushed back. I doubt he ever rode his bicycle far dressed like that. He looks as if he is ready for the dancehall, not for the wind. He has a touch of swagger about him that he kept to the end of his life. Some of the others have taken trouble to look well in the picture too, perhaps anticipating that it will be framed and will hang on the wall at home. The man standing beside him is posing too, his collar turned up, a cigarette hanging limply from his mouth. He's thinking he might get round to lighting it one of these days.

Some of the men have no bicycle with them but most are standing beside their machines, holding them indifferently with one hand. One has lifted a child on to his and the child is clenching the handlebars and staring ahead, as if ready for speed. My father is more like that child than like the other men in the way he relates to his bike. He is holding the handlebars firmly above the brakes, as in a riding position. He has his outside knee raised and his foot on one pedal, ready to take off and step across the bike into the saddle as he does. He is enjoying the fantasy that they are all about to take off, though in a moment the photographer will say he's content with the picture and they will disperse.

Some of the men are holding up for the camera the cups that the club has won. They are little silver urns. One of them sat on a sideboard in our living room for years, the only proof that my father had ever been a cyclist. I didn't see that photograph until years after he died. It shows me his vanity more clearly than I ever saw it before, though his sister, my Aunt Ena, would still be fulminating about that trait in him seventy years after that photograph was taken. I had always thought of him as a rough-edged country man; he seemed to grow more primitive and disgruntled as he aged, but she spoke of him as a young man who preened himself, who was spoilt. She told a story about how, when walking to school, he would drop his coat and refuse to pick it up, forcing her to go back and get it. She resented this eighty years after the event. Her description of him didn't fit with the assertively self-sufficient and grimy man I knew. I think anyone looking at the picture and challenged to guess who, among these country cyclists of a former age, is the fast one would point to my father, the one twitching to break out in front even when there is no race on.

A cup base held by the Derry Wheelers marks the victory of a B. O'Doherty in a midsummer thirty-mile race from Derry out that same road towards Limavady and back in 1950. He won it in under 82 minutes, which means he was belting along at an average speed of almost 22 miles an hour. His timing was 5 minutes faster than that of R. Wallace who won it the following year though E. Dunne shaved it back to 78 minutes in 1952, and Seamus McCarron, who raced for Northern Ireland, covered himself in glory in 1966 by doing it in 73 minutes and 20 seconds. There was never a time when I could have covered that distance in the time my father did, even on such a level road, and he did it at the age of thirty-six, if he is the B. O'Doherty on the cup. I would have believed that he could race at such speeds when I was five. I would have believed then that he could have cycled at a hundred miles an hour or lifted a house, but I grew up with a waning sense of his greatness and news of this achievement came as a surprise.

He was, in 1950, the father of two little girls, one of them only a few weeks old, and hurtling along the northern coast road on the longest day of the year must have felt like more freedom than he was entitled to at the time. Yet he never talked about it and when I visited him on my Raleigh Royal one Sunday afternoon in 1986 he showed no curiosity about my bike, wasn't tempted to get on to it, feel it for size. This seems unnatural in a man who was twitching to break from the line in that photograph. Once, though I didn't see it, a boy on the street was boasting about the speed he could reach on his new bike and my da told him that the real mark of a rider in control of his machine was not how fast he could move but how slowly. And he demonstrated this by getting on to the bike and showing how he could balance it, twitching a little this way and that without moving forward at all. But I never saw him do that or anything like it. I can't, for the record, do it myself.

My father and mother met and got married shortly after the Second World War, during which she was a nurse in London and he worked at an American base in Derry. They had met in Port Salon in County Donegal during holidays at a time when he lived in Derry and she in Ballycastle, having returned to her parents for a time. He cycled nearly sixty miles from Derry and back to see her. Early in their marriage, they lived in Muff, County Donegal, until her fourth pregnancy with her fifth child prompted her to move back to Ballycastle to be near her mother.

And at some stage, perhaps around the time I was born, my father must have traded his racing bicycle for a working-man's machine, one designed to carry him in some kind of comfort over city streets, with heavier tyres, a Brooks saddle on springs, a dynamo, a carrier, mudguards, lamps back and front, and even a chain-guard to protect his clothes; a dependable bicycle built for a dependable routine man, not for someone riding for fun. He went to Belfast to get a job in a bar and, once or twice a week, commuted again to us – another sixty-mile round trip.

Only now can I imagine him leaving his digs on the big bicycle to travel the Antrim Road to Templepatrick and find the little roads through Antrim and Ballymena to Armoy and Ballycastle, to meet his family duties and plan in his head, as he cycled fifty-five miles, how he might move his wife and children to Belfast and get them settled there. I imagine that, on occasions, he cycled through the night, for he would have been working until ten or eleven as a barman, and I see him in the early hours of the morning on narrow country roads with only his lamp to catch the eyes of a cat or a fox, or in summer arriving over the mountain with the dawn. Of course, I knew nothing of his journeys. I was only four at the time and did not understand the burden on him of maintaining family life from a distance. Only when I thought about it as an adult did I see how the close run of pregnancies would have forced my parents to try to remake their lives, first in Ballycastle and then in the city.

The hardest part of the journey back to Belfast would have been the start of it. There is no way out of Ballycastle but by a slow and grinding ascent. He would certainly not have gone by the coast for the first part, for the Torr Road is treacherous in places even for a car, though he might have been tempted by the level road from Cushendall to Larne.

When we settled in Belfast in the mid-1950s he would take three sons to school on that bike – one on the handlebars, one on the bar at his knee and one on the carrier behind him. I wobbled in terror on the handlebars when it was my turn there. I preferred the security of the bar where there were fewer pieces to poke into me, but where the weight of his arm would seem to be nudging me off on some corners, not giving me enough to prop against on others. I doubt he ever rode his bike after the age of about fifty.

Neither my father nor I turned into the sixty-year-olds that we expected to be. He had been born to be a countryman but lived the latter part of his life on a suburban housing estate. He could never get cars to oblige him, and would have been more naturally a bicycle man all his days if he had not had others to transport. He had a natural complicity with his bicycle such as I could only dream of achieving with any machine. He seemed able to command it to stand erect or to roll forward at the slightest touch. He mounted the bike as it moved. This was almost like a ceili dance step; he and the bicycle balancing together, his right leg arching up behind him to let the bike tuck itself under him and hold him, the two of them moving

forward like one body. Perhaps it was in observing this kind of movement in another rider that Flann O'Brien concluded that a man might merge with his bicycle, the premise of the humour in his novel *The Third Policeman*. He also noted that no man ever ascends his bike from the right, though he didn't try to explain that.

My great-uncle Dan, in his nineties, would cycle from a sooty cabin he shared with his sister, Mary Ann, down a stony lane to the wee road that led to the pub in Port Salon. I suspect that a life like that is the destiny my father missed and that he would have been content in it. The lesson of his experience is never to have more children than you can arrange on a bicycle around you. This would also have solved the problem of having to drive their mother to work, for if you don't have a large family and need a car, a cycling barman's wages will cover every need.

For a working man with a car, a bicycle becomes a hobby, if he has time for it. His travelling to work no longer keeps him fit and trim so he must find extra time in which to maintain his body. The sight of a propped bicycle at the cottage gable was not a challenge to my uncle Dan to improve himself, it was just a vehicle, the best he could manage, hardly as well shaped to the terrain of Donegal as he was himself, but then is anything?

My father retained the traces of his lost life by keeping dogs, and growing potatoes and beans in his Belfast garden. Born to the hills and the narrow roads, a different kind of life had come over him suddenly. He started having children in his mid-thirties and had six before his mid-forties. One of his responsibilities, as he saw it, was to spare them the bicycle which, by then, was nothing more than a poor man's way of getting about.

I grew up without ever owning a bicycle because my father had refused to buy me one on the argument that the roads of Belfast in the 1950s and '60s were just too dangerous. I acquired my early competencies by borrowing bicycles from friends. This meant that the machines I learnt on were rarely the right size for me. I did not go through the early childhood norm of playing on a little bicycle with stabilisers that could be raised and removed without me noticing that I was riding without them. Once my father saw me looking enviously at one of those toys. This was surely the answer to his fear that we would hurt ourselves. He scoffed, 'If you want to learn to ride a bike, do it properly, not on one of those stupid things.'

And he did try to teach me one day on his own bike, walking behind, promising to hold on and keep me steady and then letting go to prove that I didn't need him. I suppose he did this for amusement on a Sunday afternoon, or maybe he had thought briefly of buying me a bike or letting me use his before the notion waned. Perhaps he had lowered the saddle. No, I rode astride the bar itself and he held the saddle and walked behind me to keep the bike upright. The trick – as I well knew – was for him to remove his guiding hand imperceptibly but I couldn't let him do that and braked and jumped off every time he tried it.

Maybe it was the ineptitude that he saw in me then that forever persuaded him that I would always be safer walking. So I have no idea how I learnt to ride a bike or whose bike I acquired that skill on. But you can't keep children off bicycles. Recent statistics that news programmes made much of was that ten per cent of all children never ride a bicycle. This was cited as a shocking disclosure, evidence of the confining influence of the bedroom computer. Yet this darker vision of lost play still means that ninety per cent of all children at some time do cycle. There is hardly anything in our lives, bar the television, that is as ubiquitous as the bicycle, though it may only be gathering dust and rust in the yard.

Truly, how many people could not lay their hands on a bicycle if they wanted to? Even when I didn't own bicycles I rode them, borrowed them whenever my purposes required them. Flann O'Brien's vision of hell is a state in which only bicycles have meaning. 'Is it about a bicycle?' asks the station sergeant of every visitor. It is beyond his comprehension that anyone would have any other concern. Hell is a velocentric universe. The truth about bicycles is that, in our universe, they are never at the centre but they have a place in all our lives.

So, though I grew up with a father who was himself at least half-bicycle, I learned almost nothing about cycling from him, beyond one lesson and the advice not to bother. There were no bicycles other than his in our house when we were children. Later, my younger brother had a little tricycle with the pedals fixed to the axle of the front wheel. It was almost impossible to steer it for you had to work with your hands against the pressure of your feet. At twelve years old I wasn't allowed on it anyway because I was too big for it and they said I would break it – which I doubted. But my desire to ride it must have derived from a sense that I had not yet had enough experience on wheels. My body twitched to be rolling. I was deprived and still small enough not to worry that the bigger boys would mock me for wanting to play on a baby's toy.

I grew up with a perpetual sense of deprivation, of needing a bike and not having one of my own, abusing friendships to borrow bikes and feigning friendship to get access. I gathered what knowledge and experience I could by pleading and bargaining with friends and neighbours for a 'spin' on a bike that would be another boy's most prized possession. I would promise to have it back in an hour and be gone for the whole afternoon.

I refined my balance on big ladies' bikes, without the bar, plodding round on the long pedals while stretching up to reach the handlebars. On men's bikes I risked my potential progeny and all future comfort if I slid from a high saddle. Sometimes I had to sit astride the bar itself to reach the pedals. On smaller bikes I would give myself room to stretch my legs by sitting behind the saddle on the carrier. Sometimes I could sit high on the seat and pedal only on the upturn, losing all contact for half the turn, and hooking with my toe the next pedal rising to help complete the circle. I learnt these tricks by watching other boys perform them, so I was not uniquely ill-provided for among cycling children at that time. Indeed we were all trick cyclists because we never had bicycles that were the right size for us. And we had tricks for making a dull old bike sound like it had an engine. You took a piece of card like the front of a cigarette packet and slotted it on to the stays of the mudguard, brushing the spokes so that it went tak-a-tak when the wheel turned and more shrilly the faster you pedalled.

And I often fell off. Sometimes I braked suddenly and went over the handlebars. Sometimes I crashed into ditches to save myself when the brakes failed. My earliest reflections on the nature of consciousness come from the discovery that as you leave the saddle and go into the air you find time slowing down. I had only one real focus in my efforts and that was to rattle downhill at speed. I lived near the foot of Black Mountain and some of the roads closer to the main slope were steep enough to provide the exhilaration of wind and danger. I would puff my way up Shaw's Road confident that the harder it was to get to the top the faster I would come soaring back. Most of the bikes I rode as a boy had no gears – or to be exact, just one gear – so the accepted way of breasting a steep hill was to get off and push. Later, Kennedy Way was built and provided a clear run from the Upper Springfield Road, actually on the mountain proper, to the bottom of Stockman's Lane, though with annoying roundabouts to break the momentum. When the tarmac was fresh and smooth I could gain dizzying speeds and yet feel strangely safe on that wide, even curve, though on a hot day you would hear the rubber unsticking from the molten surface as you glided over it.

There was another legendary steep hill at Hannahstown which some boys boasted of having ridden down. I didn't believe that it was possible to set out on a gradient so close to vertical and safely maintain a speed just short of a plummet.

Certainly no brakes I had ever known on a bicycle would have enabled a rider to stop at the junction, so the thrill of the ride was always going to include the danger of being hit by a car at the crossroads.

Another dangerous hill that was shorter and nearer home was Slieveban Drive. It was a favourite street for daring kids on improvised guiders: strips of wood between axles on pram wheels, often with little rings filled with ball bearings for lower rear wheels. Some of the fathers had probably been able to pinch these from a factory. They would fashion a rear axle out of plain timber, a piece just wide enough to fill the inner ring and hold it fast and let the outer one, sitting on the bearings, spin. Apart from being slick and expensive looking, these probably slowed the guider down. I never even considered rolling down Slieveban Drive on anything, for it seemed to billow out in the middle section and steepen horrifically below. But once Terry Graham talked me into sitting on his handlebars and took off from the top on a suicidal run. We wobbled until we found our momentum, then we were being carried not by the effort of his pedalling but by gravity, helplessly, in a sinking, screaming whoosh. The best Terry could do was steer and weave, taking us into Slievegallion Drive where an incline slowed us before we joined the traffic of the main road and stopped. I had accepted from the start that I was at the mercy of chance and I was surprised as well as relieved to be alive at the end. The experience was akin to falling off a mountain and rolling at random to wherever friction and gravity would stop me.

Cycling for a boy was for exhilaration then, not for commuting, though some had bikes to get them to school. I walked a couple of miles and back every day so a bike would have helped. No one rode far. We were never tempted to travel long distances but would be content to cycle to Musgrave Park Hospital just a mile or two down the road and ride circuits of the car park for hours on summer evenings.

In time I learned to use the different gearing systems, the

Sturmey Archer and the derailleur of racing bikes. To me, a bike was a racer if it had drop handlebars. I could not work out why any cyclist would prefer such an awkward shape. The down curve of the handles simply exacerbated the problems of riding an oversized bicycle. Still, I knew they were a challenge that had to be accepted.

And when I had to cover for my accidents and return a bicycle as I had received it, I learned to mend machines. I once had to take a Carlton to Stone's at the Markets to have a buckled wheel improbably corrected, just by being spun on an improvised axle and having its spokes tightened by a little gadget between a man's fingers, so small he might have been demonstrating a conjuring trick. What had seemed to me to be the ruination of an expensive bicycle, and the burden of guilt and shame, turned out to be a problem that could be solved for pocket money, and a clue that future disasters might also be manageable.

Kate and Anne McGarrigle sang; 'Some say the heart is just like a wheel; if you bend it, you can't mend it.' They were wrong about the wheel.

3 The geometry would be all wrong for you

In 1983, at the age of thirty-two, I returned to Belfast from Libya and lived for a time in a shared house in Dunluce Avenue, a street beside the City Hospital that housed students and nurses in big three-storey Victorian terraces that had originally been built for prosperous upper middle-class families. I was taking my bearings and wondering what work I might do if my savings ran out. I had not thought much of acquiring a bicycle but, in a way, I was ripe for the suggestion. I still hadn't a driving licence and, retaining some of my old hippy ways, I indulged a fantasy that I might live a simple life and avoid the burden and the danger.

I had been out of Belfast for much of the previous ten years. Most of that time I hadn't even enough of my own money to buy a bicycle. I had spent four years in northern India where the terrain is as flat as a tabletop. There the bicycle was the standard vehicle for the poor family. The most efficient machine in the conditions was a heavy black Hercules bike. On level ground, its weight provided momentum and stability, handy when your wife is trotting to catch up after traffic lights and jumps back on to the carrier, especially if she is holding a baby. In Libya I was either based in a work camp or travelling with a team in a long Peugeot estate. The only bicycle I had access to was a boring exercise bike in the gym. While working there my European base was the home of my girlfriend Celine in Geneva. Sometimes when I was on leave we would take a couple of old bikes for a spin from the village where she lived on the French border, round the country roads or down to Lake Geneva.

There was an architect called Toby living in the Dunluce Avenue house. It was a ramshackle and bohemian terrace house where people from different types of life might meet and mingle, people who would not otherwise have found themselves close together; some were focused professionals, others were more relaxed about their commitments to career advancement and self-improvement. I was evolving into a low-paid freelance journalist, with little desire to be a full-time worker, institutionalised and salaried. Once I did an article on incomes in the service industries and found that I would have been better off financially as an office cleaner or a student nurse than as the investigative reporter bemoaning how bad their terms were.

I never asked Toby why he lived so cheaply; he drove a smart car, something longer and sleeker than was really necessary for negotiating the city centre and the Newtownards Road. And he told me his Peugeot bicycle cost a fortune. He loved the bike and kept it in his bedroom. There he could polish the frame and tend to the bits that gathered muck and grease.

Some days I saw Toby, in a red sweatshirt and black Lycra shorts, manoeuvring his bicycle downstairs to the front door, with one arm through the frame, trying to keep the big wheels away from the wallpaper. My eyes may have widened with interest. He said, 'Get one yourself and we'll go for a ride – not that kind of ride, fuck off.' We were compatible in our sense of humour. Toby looked Latin and lithe and spoke often in loud bawdy snorts. He was looking for a riding partner. In the coming weeks we drank together a few times and he raved about his bicycle. He said he would take me to Dave Kane's bike shop on the Newtownards Road and help me buy one for myself. The bike he rode was a racer. 'The geometry would be all wrong for you,' he said. He was a stylish cyclist and I wasn't attracted to tight jumpers and padded shorts, but I sensed that for Toby the picture of himself flashing past, all colour and shine, was integral to the pleasure. He wanted to ride fast and look good.

'Well I wouldn't be into lycra and padded shorts,' I said.

'You might change your mind later. You can feel a bit raw without them.' He picked out a bike for me that looked a bit like a racer but had heavier tyres and a longer wheelbase, the frame designed to stretch them further apart. 'Perfect,' he said. 'Pay the man.' So I did.

The Saturday after we went out together for the first time. 'No distance at all,' he said. 'Just out to Greyabbey and back.' I gasped at the suggestion – that would be a trip of over thirty-five miles – but he assured me that on a nice bike like the one I now owned, this would be no trouble at all. The point was to break the habit of thinking that bikes were for short journeys of, at most, five miles. That was how most people used their bike. It wasn't too hard at first. Toby set a casual pace for me. He explained second wind. 'Sometimes you feel beaten after a mile yet after ten miles you feel you could go all day.' And he explained that you have to eat. 'It's fuel. Same as petrol in the car except you stick it down your throat.'

Our first fuel stop was Greyabbey for chips. Then Toby suggested we go on to Millisle and we did, crossing the penin-sula on the Carrowdore Road, taking us even further from home. I remembered Millisle from teenage adventures without a bike. I looked out for the caravan park where I had holidayed with a girlfriend. On the way back to Belfast, along the coast, I began to feel I had seriously overreached my physical range. 'We'll stop in Bangor,' Toby assured me.

He pumped his pedals in front of me with his shiny black arse in the air, now beginning to feel that this was a respectable jaunt. We stopped at his mother's house for tea and buttered scones. I was working up to suggesting we take the train for the rest of the way. After Bangor my legs felt like jelly. I had to get by, using them as little as possible, rolling down hills, almost slumped over the bar, climbing again slowly in the very lowest gear which had previously felt too lacking in traction to give any pleasure or sense of achievement. Toby pumped on ahead but stopped every few miles to wait and check that I was okay.

This was when I learned another thing about cycling. A partner on a journey is not for company. You can both be alone most of the time. You set out with another person for many reasons: someone to compare yourself with; someone to have meal breaks with; someone to talk about cycling with later; rarely, if ever, for someone to chat to as you ride.

When we got back to the house, I could hardly walk. My legs sagged under me. They weren't sore yet but they would be. 'What did we do?' 'About fifty-five miles,' said Toby. 'Now you're a cyclist.'

I recovered and became a cycling addict, like Toby, but I never quite understood why he cycled as he did. He had advised me well on what bike to get for pleasurable excursions along country roads; but he had a different kind of bike himself. Its gear ratios were higher than those on mine and more tightly spaced. Wherever you were going on this bike you would be exerting yourself to the full. Its idea of a low gear for hill climbs was about the middle of the range I had. So the derailleur arm on his was shorter.

'And why such a sharp saddle?'

'Can't a man have a little pleasure while he is out on the road too, ha!?' He showed me his lycra shorts and the chamois lining and explained, 'You don't wear underpants with them. Defeats the point. They crumple and you get friction burns. You want perfect comfort around your hole − or at least, I do. Ha!'

Nearly every Saturday we would set off together down the

Ards Peninsula, cross on the ferry to Strangford and come back to Belfast past Downpatrick. My legs hardened and before long I was anticipating our trips without fear that the exertion was beyond me.

I used my bike for transport around Belfast as well as for weekend trips, usually chaining it to a lamppost if I had to leave it for a while, sometimes just propping it against a shop wall if I was only going in for a moment. A thief's lucky moment came when I visited Ruth, a friend, for ten minutes, in her house in Jerusalem Street, behind Queen's University. I propped the bike on one pedal against the kerb, the way my father had parked his, priding myself on having worked out how to do that, and chained the wheel to the frame, trusting no one could ride it away. Presumably the thief just lifted it up and took the bar on one shoulder the way Toby carried his bike up and down stairs. There is an awful shock in coming out to see only empty air where your bike should be. What did an opportunistic thief know of that machine and the struggles we'd had, and how we had shaped ourselves to each other? Every rider bonds with a bike, so the theft of it cuts deep and the loss is more than an inconvenience or an expense. The lesson of the experience seemed to be that every fifteen minutes a thief walks past your door.

Not that I had any fantasy of the bike suffering under cynical management, like a child taken into slavery, but I was sad that my own journey on that machine had ended. The bike on which I had discovered how to ride far and cover my arse properly was going to be sold on cheaply to someone who knew nothing of those pains and joys.

My practical response, walking home, was to look for it up every side street and back alley, in the hope that the thief had got tired of carrying it. My next was to buy another exactly the same and then to fantasise about leaving it chained in the same way, the wheels to the frame, outside Ruth's house, and waiting behind a wall with a hurley stick to take the head of the first thief attempting to snatch it.

And then I nearly lost that bike too. I had no work and I was running out of savings so I moved into a flat on Cliftonville Avenue and drew the dole and got the Housing Executive to pay the rent. It was a nice big flat at the top of the house with other people I didn't know very well living below me. I trusted the bike was safe in the hall. I had enrolled to do A-level French at the College of Business Studies, thinking I might go to university. I had learnt a little French while living in Geneva and working in Libya the year before. I cycled every day down to Carlisle Circus, along the Westlink across to the Falls, and then up King Street.

This was now a routine journey for me that I would previously have thought far too dangerous, the heavy lorries on the Westlink practically brushing me. Once soldiers in the back of their Land Rover spat at me, perhaps for want of any other amusement. I put my head down and ploughed on.

Then one evening I was at home, looking out the window, and saw a young man from the flat below me trying to ride my bike in circles on the street and not finding any purchase or balance. He stumbled off it and handed it to a brain-dulled skinhead, a huge man in a green parka jacket. I recognised him as one of a group that sniffed glue on a building site across the street from me. I ran down the stairs, past the guy from the flat below coming back into the house, with no time to talk to him if I was to get the bike back. He was sauntering blithely up the stairs with no air about him of guilt or idiocy. I took the bike from the skinhead. He had no interest in it and didn't seem to know why he was holding it.

When I'd secured it inside my own flat I called at the flat below to – what? Well, at least to show that I had registered what the thief had done. He was with an older man, perhaps his father. They thought it was all a joke.

'It's my bike and you stole it.' He didn't see it that way at all.

'You got it back, didn't you?'

As far as he was concerned that simple fact stripped me

of all right to complain. So I thought I should make my case with more emphasis on how serious the outcome might have been.

'If you do that again, I will call the police.'

I might as well have started urinating on the floor; they could not have been more shocked or bewildered. 'I don't know where you're from, son,' said the older man, 'but round here we don't do that and we don't even talk of doing it.'

'So we just let people like him steal what they like?'

'I will deal with him. Now you, get out.'

They seemed to think I might have bonded with them over the lark of their stealing my bike and giving it to a skinhead; I had extinguished that possibility by mentioning the police and betraying the fact that I value ordinary boring social norms like people leaving other people's property alone.

Toby had definite ideas about what made a good bike. A real cyclist, for instance, would not want a bike to have a fold-down stand – 'no more than fucking stabilisers'. His racer was the basic machine, nothing more, perfect in its elegance and lightness. He admitted that he'd paid hundreds of pounds extra to save weight that would be made up again by the chocolate bar in his pocket. Nor did a good bike have brake extensions parallel to the front lateral of the handlebars, to enable the rider with hands at the top to brake without stooping. 'Only children's bikes have those.'

And those bikes that had their gearing cables concealed inside the tube were, he thought, similarly fancied up for cyclists who didn't want to see the works or ever repair them. Nowadays, all these dainty features are normal on expensive bikes.

Toby's bike had its own elegant adaptations. He had no tubes in his tyres. The tyres themselves were inflatable and he carried folded spares so that he could replace a punctured tyre at speed, as if he was a real racer and needed the time he'd save. But he wasn't a racer. He was not a member of any club and I wondered why. He must have had some aversion to riding in a pack but he never explained it to me.

We acquired other cycling friends who would come with us on our jaunts around Strangford Lough or over the drumlins to Castlewellan. I learnt that County Down is almost perfect cycling country, for low hills provide more fun than flat land. There was Bushy Jim who knew even more about bikes than Toby did and was another loner, not a club rider. Jim had an old inelegant bike that he had fine-tuned himself. He would grin with delight as he lifted the rear and spun the back wheel to let us hear the soft click of the chain running over the sprockets of the freewheel. 'Isn't that music?'

Jim was into speed and was faster than Toby, though he was often ill, as if pressing himself to the limit of physical fitness attainable to him also made him vulnerable to every infection. He was short, with a big bush of greying black hair. His bike was small and old but he rode at a speed that dazzled us. Once he photographed his own milometer while tearing into Belfast from the Carryduff roundabout. He caught it registering a speed of fifty-six mph.

I liked Jim. Whereas for Toby, biking was partly an expression of style, a way of displaying his shiny black bottom to the world, for Jim it was only about the physical pleasure of propelling himself forward. And, where Toby was a well-paid professional who had bought himself an expensive bike, Jim was unemployed and saw biking as a means of finding the maximum pleasure in life available to a man who has only pocket money.

We would cycle out into the country together, and just before second wind, when I was puffing and pushing, Jim, alongside me, would lash his legs round at improbable speed and break out ahead, laughing, 'Keep up boys.' Sometimes we rode up the Antrim coast road. We would take the bikes on the train to Larne to get past the boring suburbs of Belfast and then follow the shore through Glenarm and Carnlough, often on beautiful days when the sky was clear and Scotland was just beside us.

I suggested a trip to Donegal to visit some of my father's family. I met Toby at Central Station. 'You wouldn't find some room for these in your bags, man?' He handed me his shoes. Toby would be biking light. His machine wasn't designed to carry luggage. He had one pair of shoes for cycling in and another for nights out in the pub. 'Don't be a moan; they'll go into your bag, no trouble.'

I had once put my bike as luggage into the boot of the bus to Derry and when I took it out found that it had taken such a wallop from other parcels thrown on top of it that the saddle had come off its steel frame. It took enormous effort to press it back on, so the blow that had dislodged it can't have done much good to the contents of the parcel that hit it. This time we took the train. Even then, Toby wanted his bike to be where he could see it and he fussed over its positioning against the wall by the guard, who was clearly an insensitive brute with no feeling for the delicacy of this finely honed instrument. One big difference between Toby's bike and mine was that the one I rode could be replaced – had been – for one hundred and fifty pounds. His had to be guarded like a child.

From Derry we cycled first to Muff, just on the border, the town where I was born, and asked around for people who might remember my father and mother there. We went into Pat McKenna's shop and one of the family took us next door to the upstairs room I had been born in. We had a few pints of beer with a man who had stories about teenage antics in the 1930s. In one story, someone had caught and killed a rat and tried to shock everyone by dangling it over his mouth as if he was about to eat it. Someone else had cut the string holding the rat and it had fallen into the joker's face. A story like that would, of course, have grown in the telling over six decades. The road to Carndonagh was tougher for our having so much beer in us and we had more when we got there.

I woke up in the night in terror as someone clamped my leg with an iron hand. Cramp. I'd heard other cyclists talk about it but had never imagined it could hurt like that. The calf muscle behind my shin had flexed inwards and locked solid.

In Letterkenny, Toby's gear cable snapped. That meant he could only ride in top gear. And he moaned as if the fates were personal and cutting up rough, as if the injustice of this might be reversed if he pleaded and raged long enough. I'd never thought there had been much point in the narrow range of gears he had anyway but he protested that it would be simply impossible for him to ride back to Derry. We found a man with a workshop who fixed bikes, and a lot of other things besides. Letting him at Toby's was a bit like having your sister do Julia Roberts' hair but there was no alternative.

A cyclist learns maintenance usually as problems arise – repairing punctures, unbuckling wheels by manipulating spokes, replacing links in the chain, adjusting the range of the derailleur across the sprockets so that the chain doesn't come off – and in time accumulates the little tools that help, some of them the sort of thing a child would retain as a talisman or puzzle and keep for years. And since everyone who owns a bicycle knows a little of the basic mechanics, you occasionally meet someone who, like Bushy Jim, is a wizard at this stuff and some who think they are, like Ahmed.

Ahmed was a friend of a friend of Toby's. Toby had helped him buy a little house on the Donegal Road for about three thousand pounds and to move in. And Ahmed wanted to return the favour by servicing all our bicycles. Which seemed a great idea until Toby saw the bits of the machine he so loved spread across the kitchen floor and Ahmed finally confessing perplexity at how to get them back to where they belonged.

'He's doing his best,' I said. 'It's all right for you, Malachi.' My bicycle was just an edge over the standard piece of scrap the plebs got by on. What Toby was saying in his incoherent distress was 'You don't love your bike like I love mine.' And he'd been right to worry.

A week later I was cycling through the city centre and felt my foot lunge from the top of the turn, as if a rotten stair had given way under it. I looked down to see that the inner crank wheel had snapped and curled in on itself. A man in a bicycle shop said he'd never seen anything like it. 'Has anyone been tinkering with this?' Still, it only cost a few quid to sort it out and put me back on the road. Toby had had sympathy pains with his bike when it had been damaged but I trusted that the machine didn't suffer.

Over time, your bike teaches you a new understanding of your body. Certain parts of my body which had previously required little attention while I was functioning as a vertically perambulating biped now came under my notice, first in little nudges and then persistently. My wrists. Toby wore little cord-backed leather gloves that looked trendy and slick. They conveyed the message that he was a serious alpha male with a sense of style before he got on to his bike. 'They are not just ornamental, you know.' I got myself a pair like them because I am impressionable and then I found that they did ease the pressure on the lower palm where it puts the whole weight of the upper body on to the corners of the handlebars. I didn't take to fluffy wristbands, suspecting that cycling – for some people – is a way of exercising a slightly gay or transsexual self-image, but I could see that the wrists needed support and rest too.

I soon realised that most of the parts of the body that interface with a bicycle are intimate. Take care or you acquire a reluctant urethra. With the wrong saddle or poor positioning, a day on your bike translates into a persistent pressure on the undercarriage of your penis that leaves it disinclined to relax and allow you to pee. This can have consequences for your sexual comfort too. 'Oh yes,' said Toby cheerfully, 'some cyclists find themselves completely impotent. The consolation is that if your cock feels like a whipped snake, then a shag is the last thing you want anyway. Ha!'

The only other field of activity in which I have encountered discussion of the perineum is yoga. This is the flesh you sit on, between the lower orifices. In yoga it is regarded as the secret home of the coiled serpent, kundalini. In cycling, it is the bit that meets the saddle and which must sustain most pressure and friction. It is also where a lot of your body sweat ends up and sweat is not a lubricant. 'You've seen nappy rash, haven't you? Well that's what it is.' Toby's protection against a rash was his chamois-lined lycra shorts and Vaseline.

And you can still find discussion of these problems on the Internet forums. Here is a cyclist describing his difficulties with a saddle of a popular make. 'It became increasingly painful to sit on the large face of the saddle that creates the hammock effect of each sit bone, protruding the centre of the saddle against the middle penile area that should obviously be avoided.' For a man, the elementary induction into serious cycling that you may get from a dealer must be similar to the way a woman feels at her first consultation with her gynaecologist.

Toby's other advice was that the firm saddle was better than a soft one. 'Makes sense really. It's like wearing knickers under your shorts. Anything that creases against the skin will bring you grief.' My father's bike had an old Brooks leather saddle which had cracked with ageing and lack of use after he'd stopped rubbing grease into it. In later years he pulled a beret over it, improvising a woollen cushion. Toby, however, pumped the roads in front of me, confident that his physical comfort was professionally attended to.

Another cycling friend of that time was Peter, a musician. We planned to cycle around Donegal together one summer. We met up in Port Salon. On a Saturday evening, we cycled from Kerrykeel to Milford and up to Downings, where we camped on the golf course to the great displeasure of the stout man in a tweed jacket who gave us our morning call. He stood with folded arms and supervised us as we packed up. From there we cycled along the north coast to Dunfanaghy and Falcarragh. In Dunfanaghy Peter played the pub piano to impress the girl behind the bar.

From there, next day, we cycled to Burtonport and took the ferry to Arranmore Island where the pubs stayed open until sunrise – which explained why they were empty of anyone but ourselves until after midnight. And after a couple of days touring the island, we cycled to Glencolumcille and stayed at Paddy and Sheila O'Donnell's independent hostel. Glencolumcille was my favourite part of Donegal then and, when I visited, I always stayed with Paddy and Sheila. Over the years I saw how Paddy's massive energies had transformed and expanded the hostel. This time some sort of religious youth group had the main building while Peter and I slept in a little wood below in our tent. One night I was walking down the hill when I heard shrieking from the hostel. I had a wee Sony professional Walkman with me that I used for radio work so I stood at the window to capture the shrill and giddy animal noises the kids inside were making. I played the tape to Sheila next day and her face dropped. 'But,' she said, with her unflappable Donegal philosophy, 'who are we to judge?'

Some of my friends had become so hooked on cycling that they were now doing the annual Maracycle from Belfast to Dublin and back, organised by Co-operation North, now Co-operation Ireland. Toby and Bushy Jim were the fit and skilled ones. I was behind them but was more impatient for distance than some of those who called by on Sunday afternoons to see if I would accompany them on a practice jaunt to Comber or Carrickfergus.

One day Bushy Jim arrived with blood on his head and arm and asked me if I would go with him to the hospital.

He was concerned he might be concussed. We sat in Accident and Emergency, him in his T-shirt and shorts, anxious because he always seemed to be on the brink of falling apart, pushing himself to the limit. They patched him up and sent him home this time. There would be another smash that he wouldn't come out of, on the Devil's Elbow, a tight corner on the steep mountain road above the city, about a year later.

4 Love on two wheels

Cycling doesn't always fit into the life you have. For a time in the 1980s, I could integrate it into my working routine, at least by travelling on the bike to offices in the city centre where I was a jobbing freelance journalist. And it fitted with my friendships with other bike lovers, like Toby. Part of the whole joy of the weekend trips and the evening jaunts into the country was being one of the boys, a lifestyle to which I am not normally suited. I prefer the company of women; for one thing they don't talk about football so much as most men, they don't compete physically and when you fail to connect with a ball they don't shout at you. Cycling, the way we were doing it, was not racing. Where we did compete was in our soundings off about the merits of our bikes or the aches in our legs. But there everybody was allowed to win, so long as Toby won first. The bike also expanded my opportunities for a solitary reflective life. When I wanted to be alone and tour country roads to clear my head, I didn't need to take a car or a bus; I could just mount up and go, for an afternoon or a couple of days.

And I was lucky to have girlfriends who liked cycling too or who, at least, liked me enough to join me on long trips for summer holidays. For most of that cycling period in my thirties I was almost single. I did have a girlfriend, Celine, but she was not a live-in girlfriend who would ask what time you expected to be back from Castlewellan or if you would pick up a jar of tahini while you were out on the Ards peninsula. Celine still lived in Switzerland. I had met her in the early 1980s in Donegal. I had lived and cycled with her in Geneva and I had based myself there while working in Libya. When I returned to Belfast I had thought I would use my savings to buy a house; instead I had bought a bicycle and lived off the money for a year. Who's to say it wasn't as good an investment?

Celine was on a bicycle when I first met her. I was not. It was one of those occasions when a bicycle gets in the way. I was on a Vespa scooter and we simply couldn't pace ourselves side-by-side. We were both, by coincidence, touring Lough Eske in Donegal. I had stopped to visit my friend Chris who had a workshop making smashed up cars look new. He had seen Celine first and asked her in. The last thing he wanted at that moment was another man diluting the attention she would give to him. Perhaps she had stopped to ask for water. On the way back to Donegal Town, I passed Celine having trouble getting her bike up a long winding hill out of the Eske Valley. I slowed down to say hello again and saw that she was exasperated. Then I went on ahead to the top, left the scooter there and walked back down to share the struggle with her.

That night, in a hotel in Mount Charles, she told me about her mixed Irish and Indian ancestry and her life in Geneva. We travelled around Donegal for the next week on my scooter with a tent strapped behind us. Celine and I went on to have an intermittent relationship for several years.

It was when we cycled from her village to the lake and back in scorching sunshine that I learnt that cycling is the one physical exertion that keeps you cool in hot weather.

Once we cycled to a friend's house outside Geneva and skinny-dipped in her pool and Celine taught me the proper sequence of drinking with food, first the aperitif, then white wine, followed by red and only then a brandy. Warmed by that further advance to my education we cycled back to her house and slept off the sluggish glow that had enveloped us.

Celine and I had two summers cycling in Ireland during the time I was living in the same house as Toby. That first summer, she came over with her two friends to stay on the Dingle Peninsula. I was to join her for the first week and the last week of their holiday, leaving them for a week together in between.

I met her in Dublin and we cycled along the quays and out towards Bray and Greystones. Our first problem arose before we even had second wind. Celine was having trouble with her chain. It kept sliding off at the rear. I knew, in theory, how to fix this. There are two little screws which set the limits of the transition of the chain across the sprockets of the freewheel. Set wrongly, the chain will either slide off or not reach the highest and lowest gears. I had another problem and that was Celine's temperament and lack of faith in me. She did not see me as a man who could fix things. 'Merde! I knew this would happen.'

We cycled into Greystones where one beach was all grey stones. We took a bed and breakfast there, and next day cycled into the hills to St Kevin's Retreat in Glendalough and back to Greystones. The day after we cycled along the coast to Wexford. On a gorgeous Sunday afternoon we found a break in a hedgerow that led on to a beautiful sandy beach where daytrippers were sunning themselves. We sat on the sand and relaxed, gloriously happy, enjoying the rest that is earned.

A week later I joined her in Dingle. I took the bike on the train from Belfast to Dublin and fell in with a group of young Celtic supporters who shared their beer with me. I rode out of the seemingly interminable suburbs through Naas, and camped for the night on the Curragh of Kildare and had a pint in the golf club. Had I been hitchhiking I would have been a lower order of life there, a freeloader, a poor boy. As a cyclist I was a manly figure, commendably self-sufficient, even though I was grubby and sweaty. 'Where are you off to anyway?' 'Dingle.' I might as well have said the top of Everest. They could not have been more impressed.

The next day I cycled through the boring midlands towards Limerick, passing over the fine chippings on the new road, through towns called Mountrath, Boris-in-Ossory and Roscrea, to give up finally just short of Nenagh. I was a couple of hundred miles from home now, among people for whom the North was only an item on the news. I'd stop at the garage shop for chocolate and nuts to sustain me and fill my water bottle from the tap, for this was before water was branded and sold over the counter. 'Have you come far?' 'Belfast.' 'Och, isn't it terrible up there; do you ever see an end to it? We don't understand it at all down here.' This was the stock reassurance they'd offer to stave off any argument that they feared might arise from discussing Northern politics.

Toby had said that if you were pitching a tent in a field you should run the palm of your hand over the top of the grass to see if it was firm and munched short. That told you if there were cattle about. I didn't need to. I could see the cows down at the far corner. I was too tired to go looking for another field and supposed they were docile and harmless anyway. I made a meal for myself with powdered soup and tinned potatoes over a little paraffin cooker, then scrambled into my sleeping bag, knowing that the early sun would wake me before long anyway; that and the sound of a cow munching close to my ear.

Actually, when I woke, a cow was leaning against the tent as if snuggling into a lover, perhaps waiting for some response and reading more hopefully than warranted the slaps I delivered from inside, trying to shift it.

I had never been so far south in Ireland before. The landscape and the accents were strange to me, as were the newspaper titles and the subject matter of their headlines. Limerick was quiet as I passed through on a Sunday morning. By evening I was in Tralee and had a pizza, then another flush of energy that urged me to complete my first hundred-mile day on the beach near Brandon. I was fit and eager as I raced along the coast but reasoned that I had to stop before it got dark. I pitched the tent on greenery close to the shore and without breakfast the next morning took the bike up the Conor Pass, pushing as much as cycling, and careered downhill all the way into Dingle where I would meet Celine and her friends.

I had known Celine for six years by then, but she was unsure of me. That's not surprising. I was in my early thirties and had no work or prospect of work. I had lived abroad for much of the previous decade in India and Libya so I had plenty of yarns to tell but none of this experience was translating itself into career-making. And why was this man, who should be training to be something, redefining himself again by his bicycle and his tent? I think she feared my Kerouac gene was at work, the part of me that would always be content to do nothing constructive so long as I was doing something interesting. But cycling is a perfect holiday with a partner you don't always get on with for in the times you are ill at ease with each other you can be enjoying your bikes.

Occasionally we had to lie our way into B&Bs. At that time, a landlady might ask a couple if they were married before she would allow them to share the sanctity of her home. So Celine would wear a ring on her wedding finger and we would introduce ourselves as Mr and Mrs O'Doherty. I met other landladies who relished the fun of facilitating illicit love.

We cycled first to a beautiful beach at Inch in County Cork and found a place to pitch the tent, beyond the boundary of the campsite in the dunes but near enough to the shop and toilet block of the campsite, which would annoy the owners who couldn't charge us. We zipped our sleeping bags together into one big double and gambolled at times like kittens or lay in the sun reading. We quarrelled occasionally. We only ever got as far as admitting how sad it was for both of us that this happened so often, and then we would make a cup of tea on the wee stove or I would teach her how to do a headstand. 'Ah yes, you can stand on your head; but what else can you do?' 'I can ride a hundred miles on my bicycle.' One morning we woke to rain, her knickers still hanging without hope of drying on the string of the tent. There was a big quiet hotel nearby. 'Fuck this,' she exclaimed. 'You do what you want. I have a job and I have money and I can afford to sleep in a nice hotel. Why am I wet and cold in this shitty tent?' But it was a spasm of rage that passed and she stayed with me. On the morning she left with her friends, I followed the airport bus out of Dublin while they blew me kisses and waved to me through the rear window. I lost them on the Drumcondra Road and cycled on alone.

I could now meander at my own pace and didn't need to be back in Belfast for a few days. I chose to visit the passage tombs of the Boyne Valley. Newgrange itself looked too pretty and neat. The guide said she thought the elegant white frontage might be authentic. Maybe she fancied that pebbledash had been all the rage in the Neolithic period. On the road to Dundalk I used the hard shoulder, where possible, but it was so littered and pockmarked that it was unfit for a bicycle. People don't seem to understand that a bicycle needs a better road surface than a car can manage on. The drivers going past me clearly didn't think I belonged anywhere else than among the rubble and they beeped at me to get out of their way. A group of nuns were particularly irate. At Dundalk I took a train the rest of the way home.

Our second trip around Ireland came in 1986. I was writing regularly for the *Irish News* then and suggested to them a series of articles on cycling round Northern Ireland. Then I went to Eric Thurley in the Northern Ireland Tourist Board to ask for advice and he gave me a clutch of vouchers for farm guesthouse accommodation. Celine was going to come over and do the photographs. She was a published arts photographer. We asked Raleigh to give us a couple of decent touring bikes and they did.

We set off in evening traffic from my flat on Cliftonville Avenue, wobbling a bit until we got used to our panniers, me in front because I knew the road better, over the Queen's Bridge and out towards Bangor with Belfast Lough to our left. This area may have reminded her a little of Lake Geneva.

By Holywood we were getting used to the weight and the wobble but starting to sag. In Bangor we had a fuller sense of what real energy we had. We stopped on the seafront and I apologised to my sophisticated Swiss girl for the tackiness of a northern holiday resort. She said she thought Bangor was beautiful and wondered why I hadn't brought her there before.

We stayed with the coast through Ballyholme and had a glass of stout in Grace Neil's in Donaghadee, just because it was the oldest pub, then carried on through Millisle. It was still daylight when we reached Ballywalter and used the first of Eric Thurley's farm guesthouse vouchers in a farm with a hefty bull in a pen. We continued next day at that leisurely pace along the eastern rim of the Ards Peninsula. Clough was gorgeous with banks of yellow meadow flowers. In Portavogie we saw a couple of boarded-up houses with 'Taigs Out' painted on the walls. Celine found this shocking but to me sectarian graffiti was familiar, if disappointing, and nothing more than a hint to just keep going. Whose loss was it but Portavogie's?

From Portaferry we rode up the gangway of the big clunky iron boat and crossed to Strangford. The water flows so rapidly out of the lough at that narrow gap that the ferry seems to just turn sideways and let itself be carried across the choppiest waves. From Strangford, we followed the coastal road to Ardglass where a fishing boat was unloading. Each fish might have had a price on a slab in a shop but here they fell about like litter. A man threw a herring at a dog and Celine took some pictures.

Our next guesthouse was an older building with accumulated clutter of decades. Celine was always more affectionate when she was comfortable and she loved that house. I explained to the woman that I was vegetarian and didn't take meat with my eggs but she served them with a rasher on top and a wee wink that said, 'sure I won't tell anybody'.

From there we cycled to Tyrella beach, where we had the sand and the incredible view of the Mourne Mountains all to ourselves. In Newcastle the preachers on the pavements handed out leaflets and summoned us to Jesus. In Annalong we turned inland, up the Silent Valley and higher. At times we had to get off and push. In my article for the *Irish News* about this particular stretch of the journey, I described Celine going into a ditch for a pee and she was furious – she didn't want the world to know that she urinated – but it was funny at the time. Then down into Rostrevor and Warrenpoint and across to Omeath and Carlingford where we visited my friend the wood sculptor John Haugh and his wife Eileen. From there we cycled back to Belfast and planned the second route, north, up the Antrim coast.

We had to carry the two bikes up to my flat and keep them there because we couldn't trust the thug below not to give them to the glue sniffers across the street. A couple of days later, we took the bikes on the train to Larne to avoid the grim suburbs and cycled along the coast where I had hoped to show her Scotland, so close you could almost throw a spud at it, but it rained on us and Scotland was hidden in the mist. At Carnlough we found the monument erected by the Marchioness of Londonderry expressing the gratitude of the Irish for 'English bounty' during the famine. 'It's not how they tell it around here,' I said. We stayed at a beautiful guesthouse that was proud of its food, overlooking Cushendall, and took the coast road around Torr Head but had to push most of the way for the hills were so steep, then into Ballycastle. I showed her the primary school where I started with the nuns when I was four. My grandparents were buried in the local graveyard beside that school and both my parents are in that grave now too.

Celine wasn't convinced that Knocklayde is a volcano, for an ice age since has rounded the top of it. 'When I was a child, my mother told me the bogeyman lived there.' 'And did he?' 'Maybe.' Then we left the bikes in Ballycastle and took the ferry to Rathlin. In those days, visitors to the island travelled on a long low motorboat that rocked in the waves. The water lapped in and we were both seasick. We stayed a few nights with the McFalls, Kate and Jim, who were then connected to me by marriage, my brother to Kate's sister. And Celine loved it there. We walked in the 'mountains' with the family sheepdog. 'They are called mountains here, though they wouldn't qualify on the mainland,' said Jim. 'But you get to see them that way on an island.'

From Ballycastle we cycled to Portballintrae by Ballintoy and the Giant's Causeway. Ballintoy harbour is too beautiful not to see but it takes an awful puff uphill to get back on to the main road. It was a day of bright sunshine and the sight of Rathlin and Sheep Island, sitting self-sufficiently in the waves, gave a stark impression of stability. You knew from the sight of them that they were always going to be there when you came back, but they would never again look as magnificent and bright as they did in just that light.

My next big cycling trip was with another girlfriend, Alanna, a couple of years later. In between times I had used my bike mostly for going to work at the BBC in Bedford Street, where it spent most of the time chained to the railings outside Windsor House. I was working on the fifteenth floor, in the office of the *Sunday Sequence* programme. Alanna was a mental health nurse. She had a mental illness herself, cyclically recurrent manic depression; it was her experience of madness that had attracted her to that work. She had cycled long distances when she was younger so we thought a big trip might help build her up again. I bought her a Peugeot racer that could be fitted with mudguards and a carrier, and I suggested we go for a long run with the tent, down the west coast of Ireland. We took the bikes on the train to Portadown and cycled across country to the west coast at Sligo and south from there.

Alanna was a large, fit and beautiful woman, and cycling behind her I could see the drivers coming the other way gawking down her front as she arched over the handlebars in a loose T-shirt, or admiring the fine smooth bare thighs that worked her pedals. Those overtaking us ogled her tight-fitting white shorts and probably envied her saddle.

The road to Monaghan tired me a little and we stopped to flex our bodies. Beyond Monaghan we skirted the border and crossed and recrossed it on minor roads. At Ballyconnell we stopped for the night and camped among the reeds and midges on land adjacent to the independent hostel. We had bread and cheese for tea in the tent but the hostel owner invited us into the house for a drink at his table.

The next day was dry and bright, and we rolled gleefully shouting down a mountain into Dowra then cycled along to Lough Gill to camp in woods by the water's edge. This is where Yeats' 'Lake Isle of Innisfree' is but we didn't get much inspiration there.

The following day we stopped in Strandhill. There we got friendly with two guys from the North who were going round the coast on a motorbike. I wondered if Ireland is not too small for a long journey at speed. The next day we said goodbye to the motorbikers and cycled along the north Sligo coast, but after a short way, on a narrow high-hedged road, there was a loud flop behind me. The bracket holding the carrier to the bike, just under the saddle, had snapped and I was dragging the whole array, panniers, tent and everything, behind me. We weren't going anywhere until this was fixed.

We stowed the bags with a farmer and cycled back into Sligo to find a bicycle shop and get a new carrier fitted. That left us enough time to get to Easkey where some friends of mine from Belfast were fishing for salmon. I didn't know then about the seaweed baths at Enniscrone or we would definitely have stopped to soak our aching bones in a tub together. We cycled past the massive peat quarry where the land is just stripped, flat and brown. Alanna wanted to go to Achill Island. I had never been there before. 'Do we need a ferry?' I asked.

'Follow me,' she said.

A short causeway joins the island to the mainland but it does feel like a different landmass out at sea, with fresher crisper air. By then we were browning in the sun the way cyclists do, to the edge of the sleeves and the rim of the shorts. When you stand naked at the end of the day you look as if you are wearing white. We spent a few gorgeous days on the beach and got another layer of tan, up to what our swimsuits covered. We were soon triple-toned. Both of us had an overlap on the upper thighs and arms, which looked a bit like one page of a book falling over another.

And then the wind reddened our faces even more than the rest of us to produce a fourth shade. Our faces were rich cherry, our arms and legs claret perhaps, our shoulders and backs a light blush rose and our bottoms whitened even further by the contrast. We woke in the mornings in the tent with our faces puffed out, perhaps in reaction to pollen, so we were oddities, seen only in our full range of colours by each other.

Alanna knew Achill from before. I had never realised what a beautiful place it was. It attracted German tourists then because the writer Heinrich Böll had lived there and written his Irish diary. We camped at the independent hostel and ate there, but spent hours every day on the beach at Keem and our evenings in the pub. A strong sun shone all the time and a strange heavy mist sat on the hills like thick cream on a cake. There was another couple from Belfast there, hitchhiking on a low budget. I remembered my own hitchhiking holidays, standing tired and dejected on roadsides waiting for a lift. We passed them as we cycled towards Westport, proud of our own self-sufficiency. Further down the road they overtook us, sitting in the back of a car with their rucksacks on their laps.

We had a beer by the river in Westport and then cycled on to Leenaun, though we should have taken the more beautiful coastal road through Louisburg. It was a hot day but movement kept us cool. The book I was reading on that holiday was Bruce Chatwin's *Songlines*, about how the Australian aborigines mapped the landscape in song, comparing the mountains to animals, and I imagined myself a similar wanderer, beginning, especially when tired and hungry, to see the brown hills around us like crouched beasts.

At Leenaun, Alanna decided she was going no further. 'Where are we camping?' 'We'll have to look for somewhere.' 'Well, look then.' I settled for a reedy field nearby and pitched the tent.

'This is horrible,' she said.

It was but she hadn't allowed me time to find anything better. In the still evening air voices carried far across the valley. Neighbours talking about us were perfectly audible. Two women on a bungalow doorstep: 'Did they ask anybody if they could camp there?' 'Well, they didn't ask me.'

'I am being eaten alive,' said Alanna. I couldn't see what I was supposed to do about that. She would perhaps have preferred to stay in Achill – or maybe we should have taken a hotel room in Westport. But she was leaving the decisions to me and then groaning about them afterwards.

From Leenaun we cycled to Clifden. On the road out of Leenaun I got a taste of how little regard truckers have for cyclists. The road surface was broken in places and the tarmac edge against the ditches was frayed. A lorry swept so close to me that I had to jump off my bike to save myself, with no surface in front of me that I could have steered on to. I doubt if the driver even noticed what he had done.

That road takes you past the ornate and extravagant Kylemore Abbey which in that landscape contrasts so sharply with woodland and scrawny peat that it looks like a joke to my eye. We camped outside Clifden on the road from Cleggan and the next day rolled most of the way into Galway. We stopped in Oughterard where the road crosses a gurgling peaty river and sat outside a pub among other tourists. A black cow wandered up the main street and the Germans stopped everything to marvel at rustic Ireland, where this could still happen.

We found a nice camping spot by Lough Corrib and the next morning, after breakfast by the lough, we cycled into the city. 'Are you enjoying this?' 'It is beautiful.' We took a room in a bed and breakfast in Galway, parked our bicycles in the yard, and felt strangely solid but liberated, walking together through narrow streets and into shops, the kind of thing you can't do when you have a bicycle to mind.

We set off a couple of days later further south to Doolin in County Clare, with the Atlantic to our right and the Aran Islands coming into view. Doolin was like a place of pilgrimage for musicians and folk-music lovers. One day I saw a tall handsome German, perhaps an academic, surrounded by adoring young women, perhaps students, as he explained in detail some technicalities in the local deployment of the tin whistle. I got a sense that a lot of people in Doolin couldn't enjoy listening to music quite as much as they enjoyed talking about it.

We sat at the tent eating bread and cheese and drinking wine and watching the ferry making its way to the islands, which were so close we could see the stone walls marking the fields. Just south of us were the incredible Cliffs of Moher. We rode out to the cliffs and then on to Spanish Point, not a long run. We called at the independent hostel and made an arrangement to have meals there though we pitched the tent on a piece of land once levelled for a railway track.

On our first evening we chanced a swim despite a sign warning of danger. The sea looked fresh and welcoming. The danger was that the breakers hit me so hard I fell over. And that wouldn't have been much of a problem except that they were so close together I couldn't recover before being hit again by another. I thought, 'This is really stupid; I am going to be beaten to death by the sea.' But I got out with a struggle. Alanna was okay; she was stronger than me.

Next night in the hostel, the woman set a little table for us away from the large one for herself and her guests. A balding man in a white vest walked around with a pot of spuds in their jackets, handing out more. As he did so he sang 'Ordinary Man' and sounded exactly like Christy Moore.

'You'll have another,' he said, still in Christy Moore's voice.

I received a potato from the hand of Christy Moore and wondered if I should eat it or preserve it. Afterwards, Christy said there would be music in the sitting room but there was no point in staying if you weren't going to sing a song. House rules. He sang songs from his new album, *Voyage*, including Jimmy McCarthy's 'Bright Blue Rose', which Christy said some people didn't like because it was about Jesus. That didn't bother him.

What those holidays taught me most was that I was free on a bicycle, that when I travelled in the meandering unscheduled way that only a bicycle allows, things happen. You meet people; you touch on their lives in unexpected ways and you encounter them all as an equal because you have the dignity of self-sufficiency and robust physical health. There is no one who will not be impressed by someone who has reached their door from hundreds of miles away, powered only by the pair of legs nature gave him.

5 Parking the bike

There was no formal end to my cycling, no specific dat
on which I parked the bicycle in the yard and said, 'that's
that'. I never resolved to stop holidaying along the coast on
leg-propelled wheels with my habitat behind my saddle. I
continued through the 1980s and into the 1990s to use the
bike as my main vehicle around the city. The equipment that
a radio reporter needed had got lighter by that time with the
invention of the recording professional Walkman. So there was
nothing I needed to transport from my home to the office I'd
been given by the BBC that couldn't be carried in a pannier.
Then, when required during the day to go out and interview
someone, I could take a taxi on a BBC docket.

I wonder now to what extent I was judged by my bicycle.
This was before David Cameron chose to be filmed pedalling
through Westminster or other classy cyclists like Jon Snow
appeared on screen, making it clear that travelling by bike
doesn't necessarily mean that you can't afford to run a car.
However, in my case, that is what it did mean. Why else would
I cycle through the rain and biting wind if I could even
afford the bus fare? Well, to ride a bicycle also suggested that
I was too self-sufficient to be comfortable among workmates.
Cycling was a bit like bringing a packed lunch and often the

o went together. I would not be sharing a lift in someone's
r, chatting with mates on the bus or going on to the pub for
pint. Cycling is a solitary activity and riding a bike to work
n the 1980s was a statement that I had a life in which some
things were more important than the job, for it was unlikely
that anyone only used the bicycle to get to work; some raced
it at the weekend or, like me, toured the countryside on it.

And since the primary purpose of my bike was to give me
pleasure, beyond work, then bringing it to the workplace was
like turning up in hiking boots or with a fishing rod. It implied
that the heart was elsewhere. Cycling expressed an autonomy
that was suspect within the institution. Cycling didn't seem to
go with work that required a man to wear a tie and a decent
jacket. So when job status obliged one to be elegant and trim,
to carry a briefcase rather than a little knapsack or pannier,
then coming to work on a bicycle demonstrated a lack of
appreciation of the power and significance of that obligation.

Yet strictures like these in working culture changed in the
1980s as a result of high unemployment, when millions of
other adults went casual in their dress and manners, usually
because they didn't have employers to impress. When the job
market livened up, many, like me, retained the habits of relaxed
attire which they had acquired in that period.

Now, what is implied by my riding a bicycle to work? Well,
it shows that I am sensibly economical, given the price of
petrol and parking charges. There are now even tax incentives
through the Cycle to Work scheme to encourage people to
get out on bikes. And this accords with an element of our
culture which was much weaker in the 1980s, the concern for
the environment. To use a bicycle now is to suggest not that
I am selfish and insular but that my conscience embraces the
whole planet. I am a warrior against climate change. No one
can say a bad word about me.

By the mid-1980s, life had fallen into a reasonably
productive routine. Half of my work was in radio and half at
the *Irish News* where I was on call as a freelance feature writer.

My bicycle spent half its life outside one building and half outside the other and came to no harm at either. You would also have seen it, occasionally, parked at Beans and Things on Botanic Avenue, where I went for my tofu and buckwheat and a chat with Wendy about how Chernobyl had pushed up the sales of bottled water; and Just Books in Winetavern Street where the radical book selection was good but the guys were too cool to talk. There were some shops in Belfast then that seemed not to welcome customers but merely to grudgingly endorse their right to enter and aspire to being attuned to their pure ethos. I'd fallen into a niche in journalism which was far more interesting than routine employment in news reportage, though much less well paid. I enjoyed the sense of being a peripatetic inquisitor of interesting people.

And while that seems an idyllic life in retrospect, it was insecure at the time and I fretted about the need to enter a better-paid and more dependably structured system. An early effort at professional stability was a spell of six months as a producer on Radio Foyle in 1988, and Derry is not a bicycle-friendly city. I brought the Raleigh with me but it stayed mostly in the hall. Then one day, out of shame at my neglect of it, and in an effort to see if I could still go a reasonable distance without my legs and back groaning, I cycled out the Culmore Road to Muff, where I was born, over the hill to Burnfoot, and back into town. It was barely far enough to be called a decent jaunt by my standards of a couple of years earlier, but I decided that I had discharged my responsibility to prove that I was still a cyclist, and left the bike back in the hall, only to bring it home to Belfast on the train, to park it unused again in the hall of my next home.

I knew that I would have to buy a house, learn to drive, get a car, make a home. And why was I fretting so much about these goals when destiny had already set me up with a fairly cushy number, making a living from freelance journalism? I did nothing in my working day that my father would have recognised as labour. I rarely had to set an alarm clock because

I could get up when I felt like it. I often had days to potter about doing very little, and yet I was housing, feeding and clothing myself, and making beer money on top of that. If my account was in the black by a couple of hundred pounds I felt little urgency to work. When it slipped back I would start phoning round editors and producers again to suggest stories to them. I had evolved little beyond the hunter-gatherer.

But I was getting older and in the same way that anxieties about health, and the nature and direction of my life ambushed me at sixty, I was at forty confronted by the profoundly sobering conviction that I was going nowhere and had achieved nothing. Decades were historical eras for me: at forty I entered the Neolithic, the period in which the human species started to settle and nurture. It was also the period in which the species went a bit soft.

I did not realise at the time that age was the impetus to change my lifestyle but I did a whole run of things in that period. One of them was to enroll at Queen's University to do a Masters degree in Irish Studies. I didn't have a primary degree but they let me in anyway. It has always been my way to cut corners – to work like a dabbler on the fringes of journalism instead of looking for a real job, to rent cheap rooms rather than establish a home, to ride a bicycle rather than buy a car, and now to leapfrog over basic qualifications and masquerade at being an academic.

One of my big resolves on turning forty was to learn to drive a car. My instructor was Eddie from County Cavan. He drilled me on how to turn the car using the gears – they'd stopped calling it a three-point turn by then – and how to reverse round a corner. Unfortunately, on my first test, I hit the kerb and failed. But I passed the second time and got that Masters degree too.

Then I bought a small house on a dodgy mortgage of the kind that crashed the economy and I was grateful for it. I got a one hundred per cent loan and an endowment policy that would eventually pay me seventeen thousand pounds.

The house cost twenty-two thousand. But by the time the endowment had matured — if that's an appropriate word for stunted growth — I was married, in a bigger house and on a new mortgage of a different kind, divorced from the little scheme that had got me on to the property ladder.

Yet destiny had been doing all right by me without the crooked mortgage and the driving lessons and the education. I just hadn't been able to relax and enjoy the life I had. I hadn't realised that in another life I would hanker still for distant goals that were irritatingly even further off. But, then again, the world was changing too and if I was to try and reconstruct a life as a jobbing freelance feature writer for a regional newspaper, I doubt I would get far.

By this point I was eating big lunches most days as well as going home to cooked meals in the evening. I developed a tummy that was, at first, quaint and amusing, a marker of jollity and age — if thought of benignly — a symbol of the cosseted and comfortable life. One day, when I was approaching fifty, approaching another unnerving cusp, I took the bike out after it had rested in the yard for a few years. I repaired the punctures and cleaned it up and lifted myself on to it. The feeling had changed. I was heavier now but I was also the wrong shape for cycling. I didn't have enough space below me to raise my knees into. One solution might have been to buy a different kind of bike, with a saddle much lower than the handlebars, on which I wouldn't have to bend forward.

The truth is that I was no longer a cyclist. I had never made a decision to stop using the bike; I had just acquired the habit of taking the car and come to let that lovely Raleigh Royal gather rust. And in time I had allowed my body to recklessly reshape itself as unfit for life on two wheels. And I was content in my sedentary ways.

6 Bikes aren't what they used to be

The cartoonist Ian Knox, who loves old bikes and cycling memorabilia, has provided me with the evidence of an early interest in cycling. It is a photograph taken in the Ulster Museum in May 1961, showing me and my brother Roger examining a 'dandy horse', an early wooden bicycle that was propelled by the rider simply walking it; sitting astride it and pushing himself along with his feet on the ground.

This precursor of the bicycle was a product of the discovery that two wheels in alignment will balance while rolling, and that even the weight of a grown man will not topple them if the rider knows to work with the flow rather than against it. It seems extraordinary that no one had worked that out before. We had had the wheel for about ten thousand years before discovering that one behind another was enough for an elementary vehicle; before then, it had always just seemed obvious that four was the minimum you'd need.

The only features the dandy horse has in common with the modern pedal bicycle are handlebars, wheels and a seat; it lacks the device which defines a bicycle as the marvel of mechanical technology that it is – the pulley system. I try to think of any other instrument that complements the human body so well – glasses?

We evolved, for perhaps two million years, as vertical bipeds without ever discovering how the forward-stepping motion of the feet could be extended into the more productive circle. The invention of the wheel is often cited as the start of human technology but surely finding the mechanism by which the wheel could be integrated into the natural movements of the body is the real breakthrough.

The further application of sprocket mechanisms on a pulley, whereby a rapid small wheel turns a slow big one, is then an improvement on the original genius. It is the same sort of trick that was used to lift weights, changing the ratio between distance and effort to make heavy loads manageable – I was taught formulae for describing this in maths classes – but what the bicycle carries is the very person who operates it. It's not like using a pulley to lift dead weight and leaving the worker standing in the same place. The driver is the load. The cyclist is the operator and the cargo. How slick and efficient is that?

And yet the bicycle has not had the credit it deserves. The history of the industrial revolution has it that every great leap forward was grounded in the discovery of coal or oil. That was the incentive for people to come off the land and build cities. But what do we see in the footage from modernising countries today but rivers of people on bicycles flowing over the roads to work? The factories would never have functioned if the bosses had been waiting for workers to get there on horses and donkeys. There should be a statue of the bicycle in the heart of every industrial city.

I accept a few basic home truths about my motivation for getting back on the bike. I was determined to recover my health and fitness, and extend my life span. A fat man of sixty with type two diabetes faces jeopardies that only accumulate if he doesn't fight back. I don't much like the idea of health as a moral challenge given that there are conditions you cannot do much about when you get them. Routinely we hear stories on the news of people 'losing their battle' with cancer, as if they somehow failed to rally their forces and didn't measure up to the challenge. There are some conditions that will inevitably defeat you and death can only be deferred for so long anyway. Mortality is the big one. There is no point in framing your desire to be free of a terminal illness as a heroic struggle which you have some chance of winning, and imagining that you prove yourself a better person by shaking it off. Good people and bad people, strong and weak, are garnered like wheat by the reaper every year with no hope of saving themselves and there is no justice in this at all.

Type two diabetes, however, is amenable to lifestyle change. It is a condition that might have been created to give health moralists a cause worth fighting. You can loosen its hold on you, slow its progress. The plain evidence of the spread of obesity, of course, is that some people are virtually helpless before it. But I wasn't that far gone and I had a plan. I wanted to take control of something. I have done this before in my life, when faced with difficulties. During a bad patch at work, I once took up weight training. It's equivalent to what self-harmers do when they are in trouble. They manage something that is within reach, their bodies. Their misfortune is that the means they choose are destructive. I know a man who, after his wife died, simply went away on a bike for weeks. With his world spinning out of control he had to feel that he was in charge of something so he put himself in charge of a bike. That's a far better response than scarring your arm or hitting the drink, though its core objective may be the same: to blank the pain with an alternative focus.

There was something like that at work in my reasoning too, and the beauty of choosing cycling as a challenge was that it would actually help. I wouldn't have to pull myself together in the end and return to the real world with my problem still in front of me. I wasn't taking a holiday from my life or carving out a new direction, I was simply returning to what I had done before.

And yes, I was a sixty-year-old man who wanted to be young again, and that's laughable for there is no turning back the years, but I didn't think it was funny. There are culturally approved images of what we should be doing at different phases of our lives. The older man who trades in a sensible car for a flashy gas-guzzler or who sports a young blonde on his arm is thought ridiculous. He is too conspicuously betraying a refusal to age that actually comes naturally to him. He should by now be wearing tweeds and slowing down, protecting his dicky heart against overexcitement.

I was refusing to age too. I was with him all the way; I just thought I had a better chance of pulling it off if the target was to be fitter and slimmer, and to unclog my internal organs of the fat they had accumulated over the previous twenty years. I wasn't going to try and win the Tour de France. I wasn't going to race anywhere at all. But I was going to do what I had been able to do at thirty. I was going to cycle whole days, successive days, along Irish coasts in the west, over the drumlins of County Down, against storms coming in off the Atlantic in Donegal, and I was going to ride the horrendously steep Torr Road in North Antrim. I was going to recover a sufficiency between myself and one bike with a few bags lashed to it. I was going to be a boy again and, what the hell, I would be a fitter, trimmer and happier old man at the end of it.

I had lost two stone from my dieting and exercise. I walked a couple of miles every day now, usually along the Lagan where it passes through the city, or between home and the university where I had a post as Writer in Residence. That walking, which was not strenuous, did seem to help with the weight loss. I was routinely monitoring my own sugar levels as well and they were coming down. 'On the high side of normal' is how my doctor described them. I would measure my own blood pressure at home and it was good. My heartbeat at rest was now under sixty beats a minute. I thought I was reasonably fit, but the leg muscles that turn the pedals on a bicycle are different from those that take you over a level surface on foot. Before I could decide if it was realistic to return to cycling at sixty, I had to get out on a bike and see if my muscles still knew how to cope, even with a short spin.

I asked my sister-in-law Niamh if I could borrow her bike. She must have thought me inept as I went off with it. I had not asked her how the gears worked, having assumed that I already knew the basic mechanics of the modern bicycle. But they had changed. Her gears worked differently from the old levers on the last bike I had had. Niamh's bike was a racer and I had no problems with the handlebars, but the wheels were narrow and sensitive to every bump on the road. Going back to Flann O Brien's theory – that a man and his bike will merge – my problem was that I had once, many years ago, merged with a Raleigh touring bike. I had no affinity with this racer and would now have to assimilate its ways and trust that it would adapt to me too.

The road felt hard and uneven in a way I had not experienced on any bike before. I wasn't even well balanced. The most common aphorism about cycling is that once you have learned how to do it you never forget. But on my old bike I would have been able to sit up straight and look around me; which is handy if you are checking the car behind you. On this bike I just could not find a way to sit still and prevent every movement of my upper body translating into unplanned steering.

I set myself a route of about fifteen miles, from the Upper Castlereagh Road in Belfast, across to the Ormeau, then along the river and out the Malone Road as far as Finaghy, up Finaghy Road North and down the Falls and back up the

Ormeau and then across Mount Merrion to Castlereagh to return the bike to Niamh.

After a couple of miles I began to be confident that my legs and my lungs wouldn't let me down. Once or twice on hills I stayed in a high gear and pumped my way up and managed not to have a heart attack. But I couldn't get into the rhythm of easy cycling, whereby I might take my hands off the handlebars and look around me, or even just look over my shoulder. Nor could I go fast downhill or bank going round corners. I rode like a nervous old man and I concluded at the end that this was because I did not trust this machine. It was the wrong size and shape for me. My hands were sore from the shocks from bumps.

So now I was looking for a bike, and I had a better idea of the kind that I wanted. But my first big discovery was that you just couldn't buy one like those I had ridden before. The cycling market had changed.

There was a traditional difference between the bicycles of sport and play, and the bicycles that serious working men rode. This was changing in the 1980s but has changed much more since. Just as people distinguished between casual and formal dress, they knew the bicycle of a man who had focused intentions and that of one who was being merely frivolous. When I was young only the childish or indulgent owned a bike that was not suitable for travelling to work on, a sports bike with drop handlebars, narrow wheels, without mudguards. Of what practical value was such a bicycle? One pothole would buckle your wheel. One shower of rain and your rear wheel would be lifting the water off the tarmac and spraying a stripe down your back. And there was another advantage to a heavy, working man's bike; on level roads, or downhill, its weight provided momentum. A lightweight bike could be stopped by the wind.

When you started to see men cycling to work on racing bikes, even in the 1960s, you knew the manly tradition of practicality was dying out. Of course, these men were improvising on the bicycles they played on and preferred doing that to racing at weekends on the big black battlers that policemen and farmers rode. You could only afford one bike. Some men would even strap their tool bags on to their backs rather than fit panniers or a rack and let the bicycle take the weight. I still think there are few things as pointless as a man riding a bicycle while wearing a rucksack. No one wore cycling helmets. I have myself, cycled all over Ireland without one.

When I first decided to buy a bike for myself the options were expanding. This was at the start of the first phase of my cycling career, the period I was now resolved to replicate. I was thirty-three years old. It was the mid-1980s. A lot of men were riding racing bicycles in clubs. You could see them in clusters on the road, panting up hills or swerving at corners, arses up, heads down, intent on forward propulsion. Toby had persuaded me of the advantages of toe clips and drop handlebars but I had wanted a bike I could relax on, dawdle about on, not just enjoy when at the extreme of physical exertion. That meant a bicycle with a longer frame and wider tyres, a tourer.

Children at that time were going about on the new BMX bike, a little sporty thing to be enjoyed on tracks over bumpy ground. And someone was about to invent the mountain bike, perhaps for BMX-ers who had grown up. Appearance was important; you had to look good on your bike, and if you bought it as much for how it looked as how it moved then you would tend to its paintwork and its sheen as much as to its moving parts.

I wonder if my father loved his big black Raleigh bicycle. I suspect he did not. For him it would have been, primarily, a functional mode of transport and not the one he desired. It would always have been a reminder that he was no longer a road racer and couldn't afford a car. A man may come to hate his bicycle if he needs it every day and if it exacts work and discipline from him. He may merge with it well enough to bank on corners and take his hands off the handlebars to zip up his jacket when the rain starts, but perhaps he becomes contemptuous of its easy responsiveness to him. It challenges him only when it lets him down, with a puncture or a buckle in the wheel, or trouble with the chain. And all the problems a bicycle brings you are dirty and awkward.

Yet it is easy to start taking a bicycle for granted. Indeed, that assumption of dependability is expressed in the cavalier manner which seems to overtake all cyclists, perhaps as the astonishment they feel at the discovery that the machine so well complements the human body settles into glee, even arrogance – a sense that nature was defeated by cleverness in the contriving of such a device. A woman may ride her bike with dash and flair. A man on his bike now is always at play.

The big Raleigh my father rode was suited to his needs. You never see anyone in the city on a suitable commuter bicycle now, unless a woman. She will have the seat lower than the handlebars, a dip instead of a crossbar so that she can step over with a dress or long skirt on. She will have the chain encased so that its oil does not stain her clothes. She will likely have a mirror and a bell and a basket on the handlebars. Her entire range of preferences is based on the need for the bicycle to adapt to her life and activities. And that would have been the philosophy that determined my father's choice of a bicycle too. It would have made no more sense to him to ride a modern racer or hybrid to work than it would have done to send a poodle to pen the sheep.

The new fashion in bikes made it harder for me to get what I wanted. I didn't want a hybrid that looked like a mountain bike, that bounced on kerbs but would exhaust me after ten miles on country roads. I wanted a touring bike with drop handlebars, so that I could ease my back by changing position occasionally, but which would be robust enough for the streets and feel safe in traffic. Most road bikes were now wispy things built only for speed. It was as if men were now more concerned to look sporty than to travel in comfort.

Yet women, practical cyclists that they are, can be romantic about bikes too and give them names. In the blog *Midlife*

Cycling, Justine Valinotti lists her favourite bicycles as Arielle, Tosca, Helene and Marianella. Justine is a writer who teaches in City University in New York and bicycles are her 'abiding passion', listed even above her cats on her blog.

The writer of the *Lovely Bicycle* blog asserts that the bicycle is a symbol of the experience we have had with it. It must be beautiful. Signing herself Velouria, she is a tentative cyclist who has built up her competencies in recent years and attracted a large enough audience to invite sponsors. Manufacturers now send her products to review. Her entries cover questions ranging from which saddle she prefers, to how to use cooking twine to secure the ends of handlebar tape.

I think my father's feeling for his workaday bicycle would have been little different from the regard he had for his cap or for his garden spade, though he may have had an actual affection for his shoes or his watch. He was the type of cyclist, I suspect, described by the website *Copenhagenize.com* whose relationship with his bike is similar to his relationship with his vacuum cleaner. 'We don't wave at other 'avid' vacuum cleaning 'enthusiasts' while we clean.'

Velouria is with those of us who can love a bike. She says this insistence on 'stripping the bicycle of emotional and personal value is misguided and philosophically flawed.' She writes, 'a bicycle evokes associations with movement, freedom, independence, wind in your hair, the outdoors and joy. It is only natural that [it] invites emotional connectedness and the [vacuum cleaner] does not.'

I was looking for a bike that I could fall in love with, like those I had loved decades before, touring bikes with drop handlebars like a racer, but with longer more comfortable frames and heavier tyres that didn't transfer every bump on the road into your wrists and back. Every dealer I spoke to specialised in racers, which they now called road bikes. The nearest I could get in shape to what I wanted was what was now called a city bike – the standard low bike, similar to a mountain bike, with straight handlebars. I had never used straight handlebars but I had to consider that most people, now wanting them, might know better than I did.

An alternative was the cross bike. This was a racer frame with heavy tyres, perhaps perfect. The oddity was that this bike was made for racing through mud and rough terrain. Some variants were made with no gears, the users being apparently eager to suffer. Yet if you could put mudguards and a carrier on such a bike, was that not just what I was looking for?

Then I saw that Ridgeback had two bikes which they call World Bikes. The publicity picture shows a man cycling through a sandstorm on a narrow road with the bike loaded with panniers. This suited the image I wanted. I saw myself taking long journeys.

One of the reasons I wanted to cycle country roads is that I wanted to be alone. And this, now I have said it, seems harsh, a refusal of the comfort I derive from those I love. And if my desire was just for a little quiet headspace, could I not get that with a walk along the Lagan towpath, or, if I needed to be more remote, up Black Mountain, where I had walked as a child?

Peace and quiet are already part of my routine life. I think I am already quite good at detaching myself from the frets and distractions of the busy day. What I wanted now was not something in the run of ordinary respite, but retreat. I could take a bus and go to Rosnowlagh: I could even travel most of the journey for free, since I am sixty and have a bus pass. I could walk the length of the beach at sunset and I would be deeply refreshed by that. But I wanted more.

Perhaps I wanted penance. It would not be hard to explain my desire to cycle far and to be alone on beaches in terms of my Catholic cast of mind. I would be purified by self-mortification and brought to sufficient humility and clarity and exhaustion to be honestly small before nature and know the limitations of my mind and body.

But there is another cultural influence on me apart from the notion of the pilgrim. It is the cowboy. In my fantasy of cycling the west – of course, the west! – I am the solitary drifter of the films, the plainsman, the driven heart-sore lover on his horse, head down against the rain, proving his sufficiency against all the badness of the world and the snares of domesticity and routine.

I have done this before and I have never found independence and know that it is an illusion – but I have often had moments in the day, during lone travel, when I have indulged a fantasy that I am a singular entity, at one only with circumstance, be it the road and the wind.

This is, of course, by some sensible views, contemptible. This is the little boy in me who ran to the shops at a trot, slapping his hip as if it was the haunch of a horse that carried him. It is play. Okay, it is play. Is that so wrong? I look at the seriousness of children. The little boy in a cowboy hat knows that he is not a cowboy. He just wants to be allowed to imagine for a while that he is a gunslinger or a ranch hand. The children who are led by the hand on to football pitches before big games, wearing the jersey, know fine rightly that they are not going out there to score for the team. But they are asking to be indulged in the fantasy that they are part of the struggle for victory.

The boy grows out of that not by learning that he is just a little boy who lives in a house and is dependent on his mammy – he knew that all along. His supposed maturing is in the acceptance that playing – in itself – demeans him. At fifteen he wouldn't dream of walking on to a football pitch holding Beckham's hand. But I don't think play does demean. So I expected to alternate in my head between being a serious pilgrim and an indulgent cowboy. The pilgrim and the cowboy were parts of my imagination that wanted to be exercised, or at least aired, and maybe in letting them have their way I would find them to be hollow and irrelevant to my welfare and happiness, like an inappropriate lover too long dallied with. Whatever, I would be physically fit at the end of my journey and I would have stories to tell.

7 Back on the road

On the morning of the day on which I ordered my bike – 15 April 2011 – the news led with the story that two local cyclists had been killed. One had been run over by a lorry at 6.30 that morning, on the Ormeau Bridge in Belfast, a short walk from the bed in which Maureen and I lay listening to the alarming news. The other cyclist had died in Anglesey on a charity race.

It frightened me to think that cycling had become so dangerous, perhaps especially for an older man like me who was out of practice. I knew as a journalist that, with two accidents coming close together, this was a story that would develop. Even if I had had no personal interest in cycling I would happily have written an article that day about how dangerous the roads had become for people on bikes. From my work on radio programmes and in newsrooms I could easily envisage the conversation among reporters on which stories of the morning 'had legs'. This would be one of them.

By a shocking coincidence, the *Independent* was carrying a front-page report that day about the increasing number of deaths of cyclists caused by lorries whose drivers do not see the bicycle beside them at junctions. This read like the beginning of a campaign to acknowledge the horrific danger of cycling in traffic. And I knew also that these reports would so alarm Maureen that she would fret about my getting a bike and taking it out on the road. They frightened me too. What if it simply wasn't safe to cycle in cities now?

Where was the sense in a project to recover health and fitness through cycling, in the hopes of prolonging my life, if I was actually putting that life in jeopardy. It made more sense to join a gym. My only argument against that was that I wanted to enjoy the fanciful side of cycling, my cowboy and pilgrim dreams; I wanted a new toy, I remembered the simple pleasure of riding country roads and I wanted to recover it, if this was possible. I had surely skirted occasional danger back then too and come to no harm. And no amount of jogging on footpaths, or pumping iron in gyms, would give me the measure of fitness that a cycle ride could – one comparable to my trips round Strangford Lough or along the west coast of Ireland. That alone would enable me to know that I was still the man I had been at thirty. Not really a persuasive argument to try on a wife. Could I not go and play at something safe?

When driving Maureen to work, we were directed into a detour around the closed bridge, where a family man had died for love of cycling. It seemed horribly tragic that though someone at home loved and missed him, for thousands of us in our cars he was just a disruption. I went back to the scene of the accident for a closer look. I am a journalist with a press card and could have gone right up to the barrier, tried chatting with the police. I never like to intrude on scenes like this; the police should be allowed to get on with their job without distraction. That way an identification is made quicker and the family gets the news faster and the road is cleared sooner.

But I was curious too. I wanted to know what this accident meant for me, for other cyclists. The Ormeau Road was sealed with the blue and white accident-scene tape. I could see the yellow and white box tent erected over the body and a woman in yellow overalls standing beside the tent, apparently giving details to a policeman crouched on the pavement writing notes.

I took a photograph. I usually have a camera with me. I am not a photo-journalist but I do post pictures to blogs. When I studied the picture later I saw more detail, one policeman inspecting a bicycle whose wheels had been bent though it didn't look as if it had been significantly damaged beyond that. I could see that the truck that had killed the cyclist was several yards past the little tent covering the body. So the driver had passed over the cyclist and perhaps not even noticed him until he was visible in the rear-view mirror.

Later that day when the road was open again I passed the scene of the accident again on my way to the university. The road had been quiet when the accident had happened, but it was the main route into Belfast from the south and thousands of people passed the spot where a man had died, most perhaps with little idea of why traffic had been diverted away from it for hours. There were now only paint spray markings and sawdust to hint at the awfulness. A painted loop indicated the position the body had lain in. The police had not drawn a body outline like the one you see in crime films, just a rough ellipse. Several yards beyond this were little dashes to describe, I guessed, the position of the wheels of the lorry. At the corner, near the body markings, was the blood. The police had spread several shovelfuls of sawdust over this but it was not enough to disguise or absorb it. It would be clear to all passers-by, until the next good shower of rain, that someone had died here.

That evening, passing the markings again, I stopped at the pedestrian crossing beside a young woman cycling home along the footpath. She was looking at it.

'Do you know what that is?' I said.

She shuddered. 'Yes. I heard the news.'

And after a pause she said, 'I never ride on the road.'

In the following days, as the story was developed on the news, the physical signs of the accident faded and changed.

At last the cyclist's name was revealed – Michael Caulfield. People said he often went out for an early morning cycle ride when the roads were clear and safe. The strange thing about this accident was that it did not happen in heavy traffic but when there was no one around, the time of day when you would think a cyclist would have least danger to worry about.

This was part of my argument to Maureen in defence of my desire to cycle, though she thought it was perverse. The fact that he wasn't in traffic tells you nothing about whether it is unsafe to cycle in town through traffic. But if a cyclist wasn't safe when there was only one lorry on the road, how could he be safer when there were more?

Then bouquets of flowers were left at the railing on the bridge, with little notes of love and regard for Michael Caulfield. One day, walking past them, I saw a large red flower lying in the middle of the road. I couldn't see how it had got there. Perhaps someone had stolen it from the bunch on the railings then dropped it. Perhaps someone who wanted to mark this death had chosen to set it there, thinking that that was where he had died. Anyway, the flower was in the path of traffic coming from four directions so it wouldn't be there for long. I conceived an idea for another photograph. I would catch a bicycle passing the flower. I might put it on my cycling blog as a tribute of my own to a dead cyclist.

A couple of cyclists were coming down the Ormeau Road cycle lane in front of Ormeau Park, and they were likely to cross the road at the lights and pass the flower. It would stand as a symbol for the indifference of the busy city to the carnage that is a by-product of traffic, more so indeed if one of the bikes went over the flower. They didn't touch it. The lights changed and cars rushed across my field of vision in both directions, east and west. I kept clicking to catch the moment at which the flower would be crushed. Yet by some fluke, none of the cars touched the flower, though some brushed close to it or passed right over it.

The lights changed again and the traffic stopped, and cars

from north and south were cleared to cross the junction. I kept my camera on the flower and again the flower remained intact. I took a hundred shots, moved around the corners of the junction to capture the flower's close escapes for over an hour, and still the flower survived. This was rush hour in Belfast, and the road that had not been safe for Michael Caulfield at 6.30 in the morning was strangely safe for a stray flower when traffic was constant and heavy. I wrote a short script making this point, and I cropped the pictures and arranged a selection on a slide show. Then I uploaded this to the cycling blog and posted a link to Facebook. I don't want to paraphrase what these images meant. To some they suggested a miracle. But they were fascinating and seemed to me a small way of honouring cyclists who die and getting people to notice our vulnerability.

Immediately a couple of friends urged me to post it to YouTube so I converted it to MP4 and did that. Slowly the viewings mounted up, to a hundred by the next day and over a thousand by the following one. I discovered from YouTube that others had been applying their imaginations to marking the deaths of cyclists too. One of the most moving symbols for memorialising a cyclist killed on the road is the ghost bicycle. Cyclists in the city acquire an old unwanted bike, paint it white and chain it to railings near the place where the person has died. They might fix a sign to it marking the name of the dead cyclist and the date of the accident. Others then bring flowers to the ghost bike or attach their own messages to it. The ghost bike is a powerful symbol because a bicycle chained to railings usually speaks of an owner who is coming back to unlock it and ride it home. Parked safely, the bike is always suggestive of a life. You can read some sense of the character of that life in the type and condition of the bike. Establishing the permanence of the memorial by painting even the saddle white signifies acutely that one rider is not going home.

It would be a while before I would gain confidence on the road in the heart of traffic, but it would come from watching other bolder cyclists claiming their space. Until then I would brashly assure Maureen that there was really little danger for the cyclist who was alert and careful until I began to believe that myself.

I picked up my new bike at Bike Dock in Belfast, a Ridgeback Panorama, with a frame size of fifty centimetres. It is smaller than the old Raleigh I rode before. I stood astride it and this felt comfortable, with plenty of space between the bar and my crotch. Bushy Jim had always told me that the old Raleigh was too big for me, and that he, about the same size as me, was more comfortable on a smaller machine. It was hard to check the saddle height in the shop, because I couldn't sit up for long while the dealer was holding it steady by the bars, but I thought it should come down a bit and then later changed my mind.

The pedals I had asked them to fit were of a type that uses cleats, but which you can ride on with ordinary shoes too, using the other side. I bought a few essentials – helmet, lock and puncture repair kit – and ordered my shoes, then took the bike out on to the Ravenhill Road. My first unease was in not being able to see the traffic coming behind me. I simply didn't have the relaxed control of the bike that would enable me to sit erect and turn at the waist, and I wondered if I should have a mirror. But I trusted that with practice I would soon be able to do everything I had done before, even more fluidly given that this bike was a better fit than the last one.

I went into Ormeau Park and rode around a few times to familiarise myself. There is a little hill on one of the paths from the Ravenhill end. There I saw a man supervising a toddler on a trike. The child had got off to push his wee bike up the little hill and the man was saying, 'You can ride it up the hill: look at him [me] – he's doing it.'

And I should have asked at Bike Dock how to use the

gears. On my old bike, these were controlled from levers at my knee. The new gears were controlled from the brakes as on the bike I had borrowed from Niamh. Once I got the hang of them I accepted that this was a better system. I restored the saddle to the height Trevor in the shop had set for me and went for a longer ride up to the Carryduff roundabout and back, a return trip of about ten miles. Belfast sits in a valley and nearly every route out of the city is a climb – few steeper than the busy Saintfield Road. I thought I was familiar with it but the route had changed. Much of it was diverted onto cycle paths. Actually these sections were mostly footpath but there were few pedestrians to share it with and in some places I could move quickly and smoothly. In other stretches, the surface was more undulating than the road, dipping at each garden gate. The cycle path also employed the same space as the bus stops, meaning that I had to rejoin the road at the layby and then go back on to the footpath beyond it. So if there was a bus pulling in, I was expected to wait for it before moving on.

Still, kerbs had been sloped for me. This would be good for safer travel about the city but not for pleasurable momentum, given that I had weave on and off them so often. And as a frequent walker, I felt that when on foot it would be a nuisance to me to have to look out for cyclists.

My first impression of the road itself was that it was more broken and rougher than I had known it in the past. This explained why so many new bikers were riding hybrids with broad tyres. The hybrid does suit all the bouncing about required of a rider on rough roads who must weave on and off the footpath as the route of the cycle path dictates. These routes now simulate mountain tracks, not the roads themselves, and change the whole experience of cycling in the city. My new Panorama was heavier, and more stocky and solid than the old Raleigh Royal. There was a wider gear range and when I slipped into the higher ones I had far more push for accelerating downhill. Then the weight and stability of the bike felt good, but it seemed sluggish on climbs.

For a second outing on the new bike the next day, in a couple of hours grabbed from work, I set out up the Stranmillis Road, not quite sure where I was headed. The first obstacle was on the bicycle lane along the footpath in front of Ormeau Park. Coming in the other direction I met a woman pushing a baby in a pram. Did she have any notion that I, on my bike, had as much right to be on the footpath as she had? She can hardly have thought that fair. Who consulted her before designating half the footpath for the use of cyclists and forcing her to the side, against the wall?

I had to use my bell a couple of times to urge young men sauntering along in my path to get out of the way. Did they not know that this part of the footpath was no longer theirs? In this argument I'm inclined to side with the pedestrians who have had the footpaths stolen from them and given over to people on bikes. But it's an unsatisfactory system all round because cyclists would rather have proper cycle lanes or none at all. The likely evolution of this system is that motorists will stop looking out for cyclists because they will get used to roads that are free of them. And then a pedestrian will get hurt by a cyclist and we will have uproar against a system that divides footpaths between people on foot and people on wheels.

I went out along the river on to the Malone Road, up Balmoral Avenue and on to the Lisburn Road. Another cyclist startled me by saying hello when he came alongside. We were bonded by our machines. I tried the same thing on a young woman I overtook later as she was struggling up the hill, and she nearly fell off in fright.

I had yet to learn how to negotiate traffic lights and thought it, at least, best to be legal and behave as if I was in a car, stopping in the queue. You learn a few things doing that. A bicycle is the fastest vehicle of them all at taking off again. The internal combustion engine, finely tuned, might go from zero to sixty in five seconds but nothing goes from zero to five as fast as a bicycle.

After about ten miles I stopped at a Spar shop just outside Lisburn for water and nuts and locked the bike to a post, even though it would only be out of sight for seconds. And I realised that I was unsteady on my feet, hungry, thirsty and a little jaded, even delirious. Had my blood sugar levels gone through the floor? My normal problem was that they were too high. None of these sensations were obvious when I had had momentum on the bike but I was as disorientated now as I would have been when drunk.

So I guzzled some water and ate a bag of nuts and sat on a wall by my bike to watch the traffic flow until I was more grounded again. I would have to watch out for the danger of this happening again. I then cycled into Lisburn and along the humpy Hillhall Road, back towards Belfast.

I was still getting the hang of the gears and found that the top one was really powerful. I would not be using it often. When it clicked into place I would get the thrill of potential, a sense of control like a rush. But it was a windy day so my momentum downhill dissipated almost immediately I got to the bottom and I had to rush down the gears to find the traction to keep going or be defeated by the gradient. Though the universe is trillions of carousels, and everything spins, gravity is boss, which means just that we are all just falling. And you're never more part of that than when you are careering downhill on your own two wheels. So it feels entirely unjust and unnatural that you should lose momentum – the stars don't – and have to struggle out of the valley and uphill on the other side. That is the burden of being human and individual.

A danger here was that the very low gear felt like water under my feet and the bike wavered dangerously because I didn't have the same control over it as I had had in high gear. And at this stage I wasn't taking in much of my surroundings either; I was thinking too much about how the bike responded to me, and wondering how close the car behind was and if he had really needed to beep at me so urgently. This was beautiful drumlin country in May, with the hawthorn out and the high grasses waving and glossy in the sunlight. But I had to remind myself to notice.

More easy to spot were the dead animals at the roadside. I saw one huge badger, a darker brown than those I had seen before. I wondered if it had been hit by a car or trapped and then dumped there. It is strange that dead badgers always seemed to be tidily placed at the verge, though I have often seen them on the road between Donegal and Ballybofey, squashed flat by the traffic, where they haven't learnt yet that their traditional route across the bogland has been intersected by lethal human traffic.

People noticed me though. At Dunmurry a group of boys shouted abuse at me. Someone in a car on the Hillhall Road shrieked at me as he overtook, presumably in the hope of unnerving me and making me fall off. When the car was far enough ahead for the driver to see me clearly in his mirror I gave him the two-fingers salute, then thought perhaps I shouldn't have done. What if he stopped and challenged me? Or he might even feel embarrassed by his passenger's stupid behaviour, in which case he was the wrong one to rebuke.

At one point on the Lisburn Road I heard sirens behind me. In a car I would have checked my mirror and moved aside as quickly as possible to make way for an ambulance or the police. On a bicycle I felt this had nothing to do with me, yet when a car overtook me and pulled in I realised that I had been the obstruction. The car could not turn towards the kerb until he had got far enough ahead of me not to knock me over or risk me careering into the back of him. A case was building for the use of a mirror on the bike.

A few days passed before I had a chance to get out again for a decent spin. The weather forecast said that the afternoon would be mostly dry. The dark clouds shifting from the other side of Black Mountain made me doubt that. But I wouldn't mind a little rain: I reasoned that an essential part of my cycling would be facing into stormy weather on hills far from home so I thought I had better get used to it. I didn't have rainproof cycling gear yet. I went out in open-toe sandals for their better grip on the pedals, a leather jacket, ordinary cotton trousers, rolled up to under the knee for want of bicycle clips, and a light helmet.

I wanted to avoid the steep climb out of Belfast to Carryduff so I crossed to the east through Rosetta towards the Newtownards Road. At North Road I saw the option of taking the Comber Greenway – a meandering seven-mile section of the National Cycle Network that runs along the old Belfast to Comber railway line – and having a level uncluttered path but that wasn't the exercise I needed. I had to familiarise myself with traffic and awkward junctions. The rain was getting steadier. I had a raincoat in my pannier and should have stopped to put it on then if it was to make any difference to my comfort but I procrastinated until there was no point.

There was no cycle lane on the Newtownards Road so I took my chances with the cars and they took care to avoid me. Twice on this trip I faced that strange phenomenon of abuse from young people. The first was from two teenage girls in school uniform at a bus stop who shouted some mockery at me. The second, on the way back, came from two young men in a car who beeped at me and then drew alongside to yell wordless monkey sounds.

This doesn't mean much but since it appeared to be a regular feature of the cycling experience I felt I should try to understand it, explain it to myself so that I was not puzzled or disturbed by it. Some young people obviously think that a man on a bike is ludicrous and, by virtue of that, contemptible. Maybe it has something to do with the age and demeanour of the man on the bike. I have a grey beard. They might think that my facial hair combined with a cycling helmet looks a bit ill considered, and being so concerned to be beautiful and 'cool' themselves, they just wonder at another whose priorities are different. But the spontaneous sneer at a man with a beard on a bike suggests that they don't consider and reflect on what they see; they react to it as they would to an outrage, an appalling oddity, an affront.

This happens also when I go out in winter with a hat on. Young people generally observe the rule that one should never wear a hat or an overcoat or carry an umbrella. It is common to see children carrying their school blazers in the rain. There is even the prescribed manner for draping it in front of you, a proper way to hold it under the collar, almost like a matador's cloak or a banner presented to the world. I have no idea where children acquire styles like this. I have a big fur hat from Canada that once belonged to a racoon. It attracts laughter and abuse from people of the same generation, of both sexes.

Were I a more vulnerable older person, I might find these responses humiliating and painful; I might try to tailor my image and behaviour to the requirements of humour and prejudice and live my life differently. I might not go out on my bike. I might avoid places where young people might see me. There are probably other older people who do protect themselves from hurtful mockery by trying to make themselves invisible.

Yet, as I profess to be bewildered by this, I recall that when I was a boy I had a repertoire of jokes for shouting at cyclists too. 'Hey mister, your back wheel's catching up with your front.' Or I would just try to unsettle a cyclist by pointing at a wheel and shouting 'puncture!' And then laugh when he stopped to check, confirming my power over him.

So some young people are mischievous and silly and have little sense of how predictable and unimpressive their attacks are on those they regard as odd. They will advertise their own celebration of conformity by pointing out those who are different, and rebuke them for getting out of line. They will imagine that conformity to image and conception is cool, though this amounts to bragging about their own lack of imagination. I don't remember that I experienced much of this kind of attention when I cycled when I was younger, before I had a greying beard, nor does it seem to happen as much now, so perhaps what they were reacting to was my obvious uneasiness on the new bike; maybe I looked to them like a ridiculous old man on a child's toy. Maybe they could read in my demeanour that I was trying to be younger and fitter than I was.

Anyway, it was thoughts like this that engaged my mind when it floated free as I passed Stormont and turned towards Comber and then to Gransha. The rain seemed heavier when I went faster, naturally enough. It wasn't beating against me; I was beating against it. My handlebars were getting slippery but I was no longer cold, not even in my sandalled feet – ah, that's what they were laughing at! And the road to Gransha goes over three steep drumlins. I could get up them when I got into very low gear in time not to lose momentum but once had to get off and then was astonished at how steep the hill behind me actually was. I rolled down the drumlins tentatively, not trusting the bike to brake well at speed on the wet surface. And I began to think I had been stupid to come so far and leave myself dependent on my own strength and this bike to get me home in the rain with my clothes now wet through.

The brown leather of my jacket was darkened. My glasses were spattered, so I couldn't even see clearly and if I fell off and hurt myself or took a puncture I would face huge discomfort in this weather trying to save myself. But I inched downhill into Dundonald and on to the Knock Road, which is where the boys in the car took such pleasure in the sight of me.

Now the urgency to get home was greater than my worries about traffic; I claimed my place on the road and ploughed on. I even got into a strong confident stride, right in the heart of the traffic, round the roundabout on the Cregagh Road, into the quieter road past the rugby ground. I waved to my smiling neighbours as I rolled up the street in the rain and dismounted on to wobbly legs in front of my own house.

Next evening I went out for a training run on the bike but, at my garden gate, looked up at the sky and saw huge banks of dark cloud crouching over Black Mountain, threatening the whole city. So I went and toured the park. At first this felt like cheating. When I set out away from home on a bicycle I am often tempted to go just a little further every time the clock or common sense tells you that it's time to turn for home. A few circuits wouldn't have that stretching built into the exercise. But there were other ways to enhance the experience of cycling in the park.

I determined to stay as much as possible in my top gear and build up the strength in my legs. Were I out on the road I would be relaxing as I rolled down hills and taking occasional rests on the flats, pacing myself lightly and looking around me. And it was evening, with just a few people there, so I was able to build up momentum. I was still not as much at ease with this bicycle as I had been with others I had owned when younger. So I practised riding without my hands on the handlebars, really only lifting them a couple of inches so that I might grab the handlebars again if I lost my balance. The point was to recover the skill of steering and balancing from the hips.

I was also not good yet at banking on corners. It seems to me that when I was a boy I would roar round bends while tilted at a forty-five degree angle. All instinct and the stiffness of my older body rebelled against even trying that now. Just occasionally I had to take care not to run into a dog walker. I was discovering how patient people are with cyclists. I tinkle my bell at them from behind and they turn to apologise for being in my way, yet I am the invader. I passed one man without seeing the animal he was accompanying, a large gruff-faced boxer. But I heard him say, 'Stay Billy.' I glanced round and saw that Billy was, as far as it is possible to read deliberation in the face of a brute, contemplating my leg. Was he hungry enough to launch at it or wondering if it might be more sport to keep looking for squirrels?

I was now beginning to relax on the new bike, to develop automatic reflexes in my handling of it, to wear it almost. Whereas, at the beginning, all my handling of the bike was tempered by caution and unease, now I could thrill in the simple movements, trust it, enjoy it like a toy rather than manage it as a responsibility. In the park, I could twirl and meander, generally play more carelessly than I could on the road, but the big fantasy that was growing on me now was one of longer journeys by the coast, extending from one day into another, in which I would rely on the bike to carry me and everything I'd need. I was integrating the bike into my life and becoming dependent on it, riding it to work and on business around the city. Soon I'd have recovered the whole cost of it in petrol saved by leaving the car at home.

My next-door neighbour Patrick had an old dusty Dawes Galaxy touring bike, though he hadn't been riding it much in recent years. I showed him my new Ridgeback and we talked manfully about alloy frames, leather saddles, the long-arm derailleur and road surfaces. I risked suggesting that we should go for a ride one evening, even though he is ten years younger than me and a lot fitter. He met me at his front door in his padded shorts and cycling shoes and we discussed a possible route, about twenty miles maybe. Anything more strenuous after a long working day might have been a bad idea.

Then we studied the dark clouds over our heads and Patrick waxed philosophical: 'If you let the weather stop you, you'll do nothing.' So I put on a zip-up raincoat and we chanced it, rolling off down the street. Side by side at a dawdle, we moaned about the broken tarmac and eccentric Belfast cycle-lane system. We went by Mount Merrion towards the Newtownards Road and found the steps down on to the Comber Greenway. There is a little runnel alongside them so that you can wheel your bicycle down beside you. I found the easiest way was to lift the front and just roll the back of the bike.

People were out walking their dogs. And not all of them were gathering up the dog shit in plastic bags. I wouldn't fancy doing it myself. But why would people here be averse to clearing up their own mess when over where I live, everybody does it? Does civic responsibility vary from place to place? Then I remembered that many of the Ormeau Park dog owners are not as diligent as they appear. They will wrap the turds up but throw the bag away when no one is looking. You sometimes find the blue or white supermarket carrier bags hanging like old scrotums from railings, or see them up trees. And, true enough, closer inspection of the grassy land around us on the Comber Greenway showed that some are frauds there too, only scooping the poo where they'd be seen neglecting it and getting rid of the embarrassing cargo as soon as they can.

There was one atrocious shower that evening. The rain ran off my waterproof coat on to my legs. Wool would have soaked it up and spared me. Patrick was instantly drenched. He had no rain gear on at all. 'Sure, once you're wet, you're wet.' When the shower passed, the low sunlight under dark clouds produced an astonishing sharpness of contrast and deepened the greens and yellows of trees and gorse. I had no camera with me to capture this but the light had a quality reminiscent of dream or hallucination. And it lasted for several minutes. But we did not stop and gawk in awe, nor did anyone else that I noticed.

At Comber we followed the signposts to Ballygowan and then turned right to Carryduff. I had been here a week before and had turned too early, ending up in Gransha, but I didn't let the uninformative signs confuse me this time. Those who put them there presumably calculated that anyone driving towards Carryduff would have started out from another direction.

The first part of the road was not too hilly. A bunch of

cyclists soared past us, taking up the full lane on their side of the road and leading a convoy of cars. Cyclists sometimes wave to each other but these guys ignored us. 'They are the real deal.' said Patrick. To them we must have looked like shapeless amateurs.

Then a podgy man in a red top overtook us and give us a friendly hello. He was more our type, at first sight anyway. But we had to marvel at the easy speed with which he coursed ahead of us, over the next hill and away.

We forked right towards Carryduff. Now we were on drumlins, deadly hillocks that can be brutally steep. I got to use my very low gear again – my granny gear, as Toby would have called it – and to practise getting into it and out of it without losing momentum or wavering over the road into Patrick's path.

At the next junction the sign said Carryduff 5.

'Still five,' said Patrick. 'It was five a mile or so back.'

Another sign a little further on corrected it to 3.

'Didn't I tell you?'

My next training partner was Francis, who turned up looking like a deep-sea diver in his body-hugging black gear and helmet. His bicycle was a racer, and seemed a fraction of the weight of mine when I lifted it, that being what cyclists do when they meet for the first time. He suggested that I, being the beginner, should set the pace but he was soon ahead of me. Still, I kept up with him for another twenty miles in the rain. But in the end he said, 'Do you think you could do that run faster next time?'

'Speed isn't the point for me,' I said, 'or I'd have bought a bike like yours.'

8 Cycling is like life

We can too easily grow out of cycling and the evidence of this is that many – perhaps most – bicycles are unused. They gather rust and dust in sheds. The image of the old bike emerging from receding water in a river's tide or propped decaying against a yard wall is almost a visual cliché. And what does the bicycle in this state symbolise but lost freedom? It pops up like a snatch of a dream of a simpler, easier, more fulfilled life, and then the muddy tide or the shadow of the house covers it again.

I tried an exercise at the pub table, when people were querying my idea to tour about on a bicycle. I said, 'But if you could come too, could you lay your hands on a bike now? Is there one at home?' Everyone said yes. And for each of them the bicycle was a relic of a life they don't live any more; that they had let go of years before, hardly knowing at the time that that was what they were doing. It's not just that everybody has had a bike; most still have one, wasting away. And the old bikes retain a beauty – or evolve into a new beauty – for a bike is redolent of human experience, memories. You see the old bike in Irish postcards, or painted up for shop-front props, or resting in junk shops for someone to restore. In its new life – or death – the old, discarded bike is a work of art, a creation out of the use it has had. In a way it is the Dorian Gray painting, ageing as we continue to present our animated professional selves in a bikeless life. It is the old bike in the yard that says truly what the years have done. And what is it that breaks the habit of cycling and estranges us from the machines that we loved? Perhaps just a slowly eroded resolve to be out on the road when life offers domestic distractions.

Cycling is like life, with all its frets, struggles and joys, but speeded up. A few weeks into my new life I was starting to baulk at the challenge to brave the roads more frequently. I had been procrastinating and the weather gave me every excuse. At first I thought I might take a whole day away on the bike and woke to sunlight through the window on a Sunday morning that seemed perfect for outdoor play. But by the time breakfast was over the cloud cover was darkening. Still, if I was only going to cycle when I was sure there would be no rain, I wouldn't get far.

I changed into improvised gear. I still hadn't proper shoes or clothes. So I wasn't using cleats yet and I didn't have toe clips on the pedals either. I had been wearing my sandals because these gripped the metal serrations underfoot but my feet were cold in them. I settled for an old pair of trainers and a Gore-Tex raincoat designed for hill walking. This was bad for cycling. I had to open up the zip from below to prevent the coat catching on my saddle every time I got off.

Then I opened the front door to see lancing rain bounce off the garden path and berate the flowers. I went back inside. Half an hour later it was dry again, and though there were heavy dark cumulonimbus clouds to the south, where I was headed, I thought I might be lucky enough not to be under them when they unloaded. Much of the sky was clear and blue and the city trees were washed and glowing in golden light.

The last time I had set out towards Carryduff I had just acquired the bike and was nervous of the traffic. This time I was more defiant and relaxed. I enjoyed myself more from the off.

I set a casual pace for myself. Some other cyclists, like Francis, were committed to speed and biked for a mechanised alternative to jogging. I biked as I walked – dawdling, looking around me, relaxed. Passing the filling station I met two men pushing their bikes and stopped to offer help. One asked if he could use my pump. I'd not had the pump off the bike since I had bought it and just releasing it proved an exasperating and embarrassing struggle. But the flat tyre was punctured and no feverish effort was going to fill it with air.

We talked about how far we had come – me from just two miles down the road – and what events they might be entering this year. I hadn't decided yet whether to enter any organised tours myself and, in that first year, wouldn't. They told me about the Maracycle. 'A killer last year; that hill out of Drogheda goes on forever.' And we parted, promising to look out for each other.

I felt buoyant and energetic still at the Carryduff roundabout with the hardest part now behind me. The next few miles were a gentle roll into County Down on a road built around rather than over the harshest drumlins. The sun was out and I stepped up the gears until I was turning the hardest one and belting along with graceful ease. Now I remembered what the joy of cycling is: it is a sense of power unleashed. Sometimes the elements are with me, as if the wind has caught my sails. There are a few moments in real life when I feel suddenly filled with a potential for more than experience has promised. I suspect most religious experiences are like that. Someone feels a sudden rush of uplift and doubts it could be anything but supernatural. Out of such elations people have seen God or betrayed themselves as mad and some have felt flooded with inspiration.

When I am cycling I switch through mental attitudes and types of concentration and effort just as I switch through gears. I move between arduous physical work and effortless coasting and it isn't always the one that produces the other. The weather changes around me so that the niggling shower might give way to smiling sunlight, a chill in my bones warmed by direct heat. And my sense of the wind changes as I speed up into it or turn a corner away from it or find shelter on a road with high trees that protect me until the next bend.

Cycling takes me through emotions from exasperation to ecstasy with sometimes only a moment between them, and the contrast sharpened by the spontaneity of change. The legs that a moment ago felt weak and crumbling seem to strengthen with the gear changes, not when their workload is eased but when it is added to. I roll a little at the top of the hill, slip the gear higher, the chain slackens then cracks almost like a whip over the sprocket and lashes round it. It is all just an illusion that I am stronger now but I am almost afloat, as if in a balloon suddenly lifting, for I am moving with the momentum of my own weight and have the advantage of gravity and gradient. I have not really earned this exultation; that's what feels so good about it.

I now felt that I had the whole country in front of me and the freedom to go as far as I liked in any direction. But thinking rationally I knew that however far I went, I would have to come back and I would be working against the wind on my return. I turned left at Windmill Lane towards Killyleagh and stopped to visit my sister Ann and her husband Eamon at Darragh Cross. Eamon showed me his own bike, a titanium racer which was implausibly light. I tried to explain that I kind of liked my bike being heavy and robust; more momentum on the flats and downhill, more stability in traffic.

From Darragh Cross I turned north again towards Ballygowan, enjoying the view of the sunlit fields, a horse in a garden. As the wind changed, so did my disposition. Sometimes I felt strong and confident and cruised down one drumlin and up another in a high gear all the way. At other times I worked slowly up the next hill in my granny gear, with little spirit for the struggle.

At Ballygowan I turned towards Comber to find the Greenway back to Belfast. I felt I was almost home when I reached the tarmac path but the wind was in my face all the way now and the journey was a struggle. I pictured myself soon rolling up in front of my home, lifting my right leg over the saddle and bringing it down until I was perfectly erect on the left pedal, ready to stop and step back off. That was the way my father always got off his bike. By the time I was in the street I was too stiff for style and just braked and heaved myself over and wheeled the bike through the gate.

This is what I had missed on earlier outings, the ecstasy and the pain.

There is a cycle path that runs near my home along the river Lagan. It can take me in one direction to Lisburn and in the other to Whiteabbey. On a blowy Sunday afternoon in May, I crossed the Ormeau Park to the bridge over the Lagan and took the cycle path along the river towards Central Station. This could be one of the best sections of cycle path in Belfast because it is quiet and peaceful, follows a river and has a beautiful view of the park and the hills beyond. But whoever designed it must never have ridden a bicycle. The surface is red and granular, some type of concrete perhaps, dusted with a gritty surface that some consultant has said would be non-slip, and bordered with rough grey stone bricks. Clearly a decorative eye was applied to the whole project but what notion prompted the designers to intersect the path at regular intervals of about 20 feet, with lines of the same brickwork? It is impossible to have a comfortable ride there. It cannot be that the bricks were laid down as speed bumps, for no other cycle lane in Belfast has traffic calming or is patterned in the same way.

Perhaps they really were trying to recreate the surface

desired by all-terrain cyclists, the ones who like bumps and shudders. Certainly, if you want a rough road to test the durability of your wheels and your bones, this is the route to take. But the path takes a cyclist around the Waterfront Hall, the loveliest building in the city, over smooth flagstones and past sculptures like the John Kindness Big Fish at the weir, and the tubular woman with the hoop who apparently symbolises all we should be grateful for in Belfast.

There were a few places at which I had to take pedestrian crossings, for instance at the Queen's Bridge, but the most amateurish cyclist could follow this route in safety from traffic, as easily as a pedestrian. At Clarendon Dock I lost my way, not knowing where to make my exit. I presumed at first that I might be wise following the water's edge. From there I got a view of the new *Titanic* building, with its glinting, wave patterned walls. But this route took me into other docks, the Pollock and the Dufferin, down big wide deserted and dusty roads. In one there was a massive pile of wood chips being blown by the wind, in another a mountain of rock salt.

At a roundabout near the exit, when I found it, lay a little dead squirrel. It may have been hit by a car but it looked perfectly intact but for a few spots of blood around the head, and the tail was being tossed back and forth by the wind. It was a grey squirrel yet up close it was clear that there was a coppery tint over much of its fur. I picked it up and threw it into a hedge to save it the indignity of being squashed by passing traffic, and was surprised to find that it weighed as much as a cat would have done.

Back on the proper cycle track, in front of McMahon's bar, I followed directions through roads that skirted the perimeter of the docks. This is probably the bleakest part of the whole city. Just the starkness of the walls and the absence of any other life made me feel unsafe. The dockland area of every city has associations with crime, smuggling and prostitution, if only because writers and film-makers like locations like these. In fact, there was no one there but myself and the occasional cyclist. It might have been the perfect place for a murder but there was no one to kill or be killed by.

The path led in time to a motorway roundabout which I had to cross to join a tarmac path that followed the shore. To my right I had a view of the whole of Belfast Lough and planes coming in to land at the George Best City Airport. To my left was the constant roar of traffic headed towards Larne.

If the cycle path by the Lagan at Ormeau was overdone, this one was in need of maintenance because tree roots underneath were breaking through. The tide was out and there was furzy growth on the rocks that I thought might have been the windblown wood chippings from the dock. The cycling here was easy and relaxed. There was no temptation to build speed away from such beautiful surroundings. The path came out by the promenade at Whiteabbey. There I saw the information sign describing the whole cycling network.

It was a bright and sunny day and a lot of people had come down here to stroll and meander with their children and their pets. Again I wondered if they had ever assented to sharing their space with cyclists but they did not seem to mind that I nudged my way through them, tinkling my bell to warn them to step aside for me.

But there were dangers that I couldn't have planned for. Suddenly a large bee flew into my face. And it didn't fly away. It got trapped under the left lens of my spectacles. I felt its fur against my cheek and eyelid as it frantically struggled the way you often see them do against a window. And my forward motion on the bike was pushing it back into my face when it might have escaped had I been still. If it blamed me for this predicament we shared, then it would sting. This was happening almost too quickly for me to be frightened but if it lasted another second I would have to brake, get off the bike and take off my glasses, or just raise a hand to the glasses and fling them away from me. Then the bee whirred louder and escaped over the top, brushing my eyebrow, before the murderous reflex overtook it or panic hurled me from the bike.

I passed a small child at the promenade wall who, without looking, turned to run to his mother sitting on a bench and crashed into the side of me. Had he moved a fraction of a second earlier, I would have had to brake to avoid hitting him and might have failed. His mother was only apologetic. Near misses were obviously normal in her child's life and she was getting used to them.

I was beginning to realise that there was a paradox at the heart of my attitude to cycling. I wanted to ride my bike for leisure, not for sport, or so I thought. But there is an eager small man in me who accepts physical challenges, presumably to counter a fear that he is less of a man than those closer to average height or above it. And with ageing came the added need to prove myself equal to men twenty and thirty years younger than me.

When I am, say, helping out with other men, lifting boxes or suitcases, I always pick the heaviest one to pre-empt anyone tempted to suggest I can't manage. Not that I am actually a strong man; I am not. And there is always another man in the group who will try to get away with lifting as little as he can; the one in the production crew who will carry the reflector while you carry the tripod, the apprentice who will bring the spanner while his mate lugs a wheel. I don't understand that type. They are too sensible to be within the range of my comprehension.

Where I contradict myself is that if I had been dedicated to proving myself physically equal to those bigger than me, I would have trained hard and maintained my strength. The whole pattern of my life, with occasional flurries of enthusiasm for health and exercise against the general background of ageing, slackening and fattening, betrays a slothful indulgent core, more interested in pleasure than in work, happiest when work is enjoyable. Indeed, maybe this new commitment to cycling fitted that pattern more than any new resolve to be a fitter, healthier man.

I had provided myself with a narrative to explain my cycling and it included a desire to enjoy it in a casual way. I wanted to carouse on a bike. I wanted to roll along country and coastal roads, breathing fine air and enjoying the surroundings. I knew that I was not yet fit enough to do this. So, the paradox was that I would have to become strong enough to cycle at ease. And how was I to do that? By cycling hard. But would I enjoy that?

My brother-in-law Mel told me one day that he was training for a triathlon that included a twenty-kilometre cycle race. He would be going out that evening for a spin on the bike. Perhaps I might join him? But I said I wasn't into speed. My cycling was easy, natural, go-out-and-enjoy-yourself cycling. That was fine, he said; he wasn't into speed either. Except that, in my terms, he was.

That evening I cycled over to his house, close to the Comber Greenway, and we said we'd just do the length of it and come back. Even to me, that seemed now a slight challenge.

When we got on to the main path we found our way obstructed by about twenty youngsters on a sunny evening club outing of some sort, and they were so spread out on their bikes – the wee hard competitive ones I understood so well, pushing ahead – that it took us a mile to get well clear of them. Then Mel bolted and I raised myself off my saddle for a bit more push on high gear to keep up with him. He moved like a real racer. He was riding the horrid wee bike I had borrowed from his wife Niamh at the start of my cycling adventure, but he was banking on bends and weaving round obstacles, like the gates at intersections, and planning ahead to be in low gear before he reached steep hills. He was great and when the strain told on me I reasoned with myself that this wasn't really what I wanted to do so there was no disgrace in failing. But the Greenway had never seemed so short.

On the way back I stopped to talk to a photographer who

told me he had found fourteen blackcaps breeding in that area. You saw all sorts of things on the Greenway if you took the time to look around, he said. I was all for that. Once I saw a group of women in a field practising their line-dancing steps.

But Mel was waiting for me and when I caught up with him he shot off again, setting a pace that would make us breathless, since training is no use unless it gets the heart rate up, and if you only have an hour for it, then it makes sense to go as fast as you can. 'Well he does have twenty years on you,' said Maureen when I got home.

Then, the next day, I talked Maureen into coming out on her bike along the cycle path to Whiteabbey, and this time I was conscientiously going slower for her, and realising that finding a partner whose natural pace was the same as my own might be difficult. Matt Seaton describes in his book, *The Escape Artist*, how meeting Mick, who raced at the same speed as him, was a breakthrough in his own development. But I knew that I was always going to be with someone who was holding me back or racing ahead. I retained an understanding from past experience with Toby that I was never likely to have a companion who would be comfortable travelling at my speed. I didn't even have the expectation. Always when cycling I would be alone for most of the journey or I would be over-conscious of a companion slowing down for me or trying to keep up. It made more sense to be resigned to cycling as a solitary hobby or at least to let other riders feel free to fall behind or to rush ahead and meet me again further along the road.

Even for a slow casual cyclist, speed is important. You have a pace that is natural to you. And if you're a wee man trying to be a big man then you're always tempted to go faster. And even if you are just a sane mature person getting fitter, you will, in time, become an abler and stronger biker.

It was time now to try a longer trip, comparable to the ones I had made with Toby on Saturday afternoons in the 1980s. I would wear my padded undies and my new cycling shoes with cleats and try fifty miles, up to the Carryduff roundabout the hard way, then south to Downpatrick and home through Killyleagh, Comber and the Greenway.

I stuffed my pockets with cashew nuts and sunflower seeds for nutrition and left the pannier at home. Setting off, I used the sides of the pedals without the cleat devices, not feeling confident yet about using them in city traffic. I was soon so hot that I regretted wearing my leather jacket but I had nowhere to put it so I kept it on. It's as well I did.

The steep road to Carryduff felt shorter now than before, just as the Greenway with Mel had. I stopped at the roundabout and gorged down some nuts and about a pint of water. I was aching in the thighs but I was going to stretch myself on this trip. I would get to Downpatrick even if the effort wrecked me, and I would get back at whatever pace I could manage for, by then, I would have no alternative.

On the road to Saintfield I slipped into the cleats and pedalled hard downhill. This felt great. Now I was wearing the bike; it was an extension of my own body. It was my shoes. I reminded myself to remember to disengage the cleats before stopping, so that I wouldn't fall over. Then I forgot. I had already developed habits for stopping and dismounting, and these stayed in play. I couldn't just instruct my body to override my reflexes. My hands expected to act first on the brakes, my feet later. That was the way they were going to do it.

I realised too late that I was falling over on to the footpath. My feet were attached to the bike and my spontaneous efforts to break the fall achieved nothing. I clumped over like dead weight with nothing but hope and my leather jacket to protect me. I grazed my left knee and lay there, embarrassed, entangled with the bike as with a lover, caught out, in full view of the whole countryside and the passing traffic. I had to plan my delicate extrication and then examine limbs and the bike for damage. By a pleasant surprise we were both fine. The jacket I had wished I had left behind had saved my elbow and shoulder.

And for all that I should have learnt from that fall, the same thing happened again just a mile down the road, approaching the traffic lights in Saintfield. This time I tried harder to apply reason to an activity which was already automated in my unconscious. Step one was to detach the cleat on my left. I would do that by twisting my heel away from the bicycle. Unfortunately that foot seemed able only to free itself at the bottom of the turn. Okay, I was rolling; I'd free the right. It was out. No trouble. Now I had to flip that pedal over to use the plain side of it, lower the left and then jerk my left heel. It was all too much, simple as it sounds. The fact is my brain had already assimilated a routine for stopping the bike and needed another automated routine to be more deeply embedded still before it could allow it to predominate. Reason wasn't going to work. Forward planning availed of nothing. Only practice would get me to the stage where I could trust cleats. So I stopped at the kerb, yelled fuck and fell over again. And again I was mercifully undamaged.

As I was leaving Saintfield I was overtaken by a young woman on a bike. I studied her heels to see how she managed. She was using toe clips and kept them down until she was clear of the town then flicked her pedals over and tucked her feet into them as lightly as she might have stepped into slippers from the bath. I wondered if she had to think through that movement or if it was now encoded in her reflexes. I used the cleats for most of the rest of the journey, getting my feet free at Crossgar until I was through the town, and locked back in afterwards without falling over.

I was beginning to feel the strain of my exertion though and decided to stop in Downpatrick. First there were a couple of big hills to climb and to whizz down the other side of. As soon as I saw the church at the end of the road I disengaged the cleats. I would call my friend, the photographer Bobbie Hanvey, and if he wasn't home I would go to a chippy or the arts centre. Bobbie was home and brought me in, and fed me a boiled egg and toast, and took my photograph with the bicycle in his backyard. I stayed about an hour with him, and he showed me his new Leica and his study, and then he waved me off and urged me to be careful.

'Och, drivers have their own good reasons not to run over cyclists,' I said.

'Aye, until you meet some mad bastard who's just had a row with his missus and isn't thinking straight.'

I promised to be wary of mad bastards and turned towards Killyleagh where some of the roads were marked as cycling routes and there were even signs up urging motorists to watch out for us.

It was at this stage of the journey that I lost the clarity of my distinction between leisure and sport, between casual cycling and the physical challenge. It was about two o'clock on a sunny Saturday afternoon in June. I had all day. I could have stopped anywhere by the side of the road and chewed on a bit of grass or made a couple of phone calls. I could have stopped at Balloo House and enjoyed a piece of smoked haddock with a runny poached egg on it. I had options but I reacted as if I had none and was simply compelled to cycle as hard as I could and get home as soon as possible.

And I was aware of that. I was asking myself why I was behaving like this, what momentum was driving me on. Sometimes it just seemed to be the lay of the land. If I was going to stop, then I didn't want to do it at the bottom of a hill and start off again with struggle to the top. If I was at the top of a hill, I wasn't going to stop and sit down and enjoy the view because I had gravity to take me further, and that would bring me more joy.

But the real problem was that my mind was fixed on my destination, sharpened by a doubt that I might not make it. The only pleasure now was in seeing on the signposts how much closer I was to completing my challenge. But what sense was there in this challenge? I wasn't training to race. I was getting myself fit to enjoy using my nice new bicycle as a vehicle on which I might cruise along the coast and savour the smell of kelp on the breeze.

If I stayed in this frame of mind there would be little joy in my cycling beyond the sense of accomplishment at the end of each day. I was focusing too much on arriving, not on going. Was I to end each journey rubbing sore muscles and feeling like a real man who had defeated age and short legs or was I to derive pleasure from the business of cycling? Could I not be happy with where I was without fretting about whether I'd get to somewhere else? This seemed almost a question about all of life and not just a jaunt through County Down.

I passed through Killyleagh where a group of young people loitered on a corner as if waiting for the world to begin. A little further on I was spotted by two languorous boxer dogs who took offence at the sight of me and barked from deep within their cavernous lungs but decided not to chase me.

And I didn't stop until I reached the Comber Greenway – another twelve miles – where I sat and ate more sunflower seeds. There I took my time to uncleat myself before stopping and landed safely. But I was tired and knew that my judgement was poor. There are several intersections across the Greenway path and I knew I would have plenty of practice getting out of my cleats in time before each of them. And this worked well. Cyclists coming the other way smiled and waved at me, perhaps recognising the pain and fatigue on my face, the smirk of delirium.

I had only one more cleat accident that day. I'd come out of them for an intersection, crossed the road on to a little hill and found myself in too high a gear. So I raised myself off the saddle and put my whole weight on the wrong side of the right pedal and slipped back into the cleat.

After one turn of the pedal I stalled, but my right foot was on a high position and I couldn't extricate it so I keeled over again, more blithely this time, accepting now that I didn't hurt myself when I fell. My foolish brain was learning the wrong lesson from these accidents.

But in time I would acquire the habit of coming out of the cleat in advance of danger and finding the right side of the pedal without thinking about it. Whether I would ever learn to enjoy cycling without over-exertion seemed the fundamental question of my life, the balance between being and doing.

I expect I'll be working on that one right to the end.

9 The tootle

I decided that it was time for a more determined effort to crack the art of tootling, conscious at the same time that determination and tootling belong to opposite attitudinal poles. I would have to be a bit more Zen-like about this.

Tootling is my word for relaxed cycling. When I tootle, I am not in a hurry to get anywhere. This is not a race against another cyclist, against my own past performance or against time. This kind of cycling accepts no challenge, other than the challenge to learn how to tootle, to live in the moment without anxiety or pressure. Perhaps this is a form of cycling best suited to the older person; when I was younger I was more eager to be belting on down the road; when I was completing arduous journeys I was panting fretfully, drawing deep on the last of my physical resources. Tootling is just being, strolling, but with a bicycle underneath you, more alert to birdsong than to the cadence of pedalling, the miles covered, the distance from home.

I would only discover the essential ingredients of tootling by doing and learning, but it seemed that the first important step was not to have a clear destination: I should set out with no other resolve than to enjoy my cycling, not leaning ahead into the future or panting to be elsewhere. So I might have a general direction to aim at but no resolution to arrive anywhere. I might go ten miles or eighty miles. I would decide as I tootled, not plan in advance.

Of course you cannot even tootle without some preparation. You need a bike. I put on my padded underpants and packed a raincoat in my pannier and filled my water bottle. I had cash so if I was hungry I could buy a sandwich in a garage or stop and have a pub lunch. No problem.

I tootled – that is, I rode casually – out on to the cycle lane down the Ormeau Road. I caught myself thrusting forward when the way ahead was clear and told myself not to. 'You're not going anywhere.' That meant I had no need to pedal downhill if the momentum and gravity were carrying me along at a pleasant pace. I turned left along the River Lagan where I saw a boat race. I stopped and looked. You can do that when you're tootling. Lots of fit young people were milling about in tight shorts and vests – rather like cyclists themselves. I thought that the boating equivalent of tootling would be 'messing about on the river'.

These were all trim and competitive people, and the club had set out white plastic chairs so that their parents, dressed for the occasion, might sit and admire them and urge them on. Men in pressed jeans and cravats shared their admiration for their children with women in big hats drinking white wine from fluted glasses. I wondered if any of these boaters ever just played. It seemed there was no messing here.

Then I saw my neighbours Andy and Fiona and their son. The boy was about ten years old and I asked him if he had a bicycle himself. He said he had and that it had six gears. I told them that mine had twenty-seven, then quickly corrected myself to say 'but you only ever use about six of them.' Andy said he was thinking of taking up cycling too.

From there I got on to the towpath along the river. This was a perfect route for tootling. You cannot travel at speed here because you frequently have to stop to let children and dogs have time to notice you. You often meet cyclists coming the other way, and sometimes, on bends on the towpath, you skirt the very edge of the river and if you skidded or collided you would go straight in to the water or, as an occasional alternative, a bed of nettles. There were some sleek young racing types out on the towpath but they must have found it frustrating not to be able to build speed.

I passed the famous lock keeper's cottage, where young families sat eating at tables in the open air. On a footbridge, a little girl with her pink bike huddled close to the barrier to let me pass. I don't know why she was frightened of me; perhaps she is frightened of everyone.

The route then passes through Barnett's Park and the path is divided by a white line to separate pedestrians from cyclists, though it seemed to me that cyclists were more conscious of this than pedestrians were. I stopped again to talk to my neighbour Jan who was out walking with a woman friend. This was proper tootling, I told myself, not going anywhere, not being driven by determination to reach any particular place by any time. 'Nice sort of day,' I said. 'I was expecting rain.' 'Lovely,' said Jan. Then there was a little commotion. Three speed cyclists coming one way converged near us with tootlers coming the other and each had to veer off the cycling path because I was blocking it. It was a tootling man who had a flash of temper with the speed boys, 'It's not meant to be a race track, you know.' Tootlers shouldn't get angry. 'Oh,' said Jan's friend, 'some people seem ready for a fight all the time.'

At Shaw's Bridge, more canoeists were packing up their kit into vans and changing, and I had to weave through them but one, a young woman, came out of the group and opened a wooden gate for me. And the rest of the path along the river was quiet, though narrow in places. Surely some people must fall into the water here. Out towards Edenderry I lost the path, and found myself turning back towards home. It might have been in the spirit of tootling to go with this but it would have been a short excursion. There are big iron signposts like totem poles painted black, but you needed to know where you were to understand instructions on how to get to where they pointed.

I thought I would keep myself on a direction away from the town by crossing the main road and bridge, forgetting that I had already crossed the river on a little footbridge. I was walking down a wet incline with my bike to the river and discovered then that my cycling shoes had no grip and nearly lost my footing. Back on the bike and tootling ahead, I noticed that some of the people and dogs I passed were familiar. One was a man with four little copper-haired dogs sniffing around in his train while he spoke to his bookie on the phone. You can pick up a lot from people's conversations just by tootling past them. But the logic pressed in on me that the only way I could be overtaking people I had passed before was if I was going back the way I had come so I turned round again. You can do that without fretting when you're tootling. This wasn't time lost on a planned journey; it was a tootle.

Following the river I could get some sense of the area I was passing through from the sounds that drifted to me – an ice cream van or church bells – and from the litter and graffiti. There was a display that seemed to be the remnants of the sort of floral bouquets that people leave at the scene of a road death, and it was sobering to see that someone had died in such a quiet place. This path took me into Lisburn at the Island Centre. Trying to recover the path on the other side – though hopefully still in the spirit of tootling – I met another cyclist, on a tourer laden with front and back panniers. 'Have you come far?' 'Just from the ferry.' He was trying to work out the best way to get to a campsite in Banbridge. 'The nearest way is just to take the A1.' He was going to spend the next two weeks cycling in Ireland, heading south, and had covered much of the country before. I waved goodbye, half regretting that I had not urged him to head for the west.

I found the last stage of the towpath on a route that would lead ultimately to Lough Neagh and then had to choose which direction to take, whether to carry on to the lough or loop back to the city. The A1 was a right turn just to my left. I was back in traffic and negotiating the Sprucefield roundabout. It was a bit difficult to tootle round that, and then I turned south to Hillsborough. There I bought a sandwich in the Mace. One woman at the till was singing to her friend, 'you always hurt the one you love'.

And I took my picnic out the road towards Comber. The challenge now was to find a nice spot to sit down and eat. And though this was a lovely country road over drumlins, practically every attractive stopping spot was someone's front gate or too close to one for me to sit there and not feel intrusive. Any patch that looked manicured was private. And while there were lovely views of the sunlit hills and fields around me, there never seemed to be a view I could just sit and enjoy. I was discovering the drawbacks of the unplanned picnic. Wherever I stopped, I was going to look like a tramp. People in cars going past would ask themselves, 'Now, why has he stopped there?' But so long as the spot I chose was visible and out of their way, they wouldn't need to fret or be tempted to disrupt my peace with a horn blast. I found a scruffy corner by a gravelly path, facing a gap in the hedge on the other side of the road and a valley falling away. I was at the top of a drumlin. I sat down and scoffed half a pint of water and unpicked the cellophane from my sandwich.

So, I asked myself, how was I getting on with the tootling? If I had been a racer, I would have had my milometer on the handlebars and I would have been able to calculate the measure of my achievement and compare it with past exertions. But how do you quantify a tootle? Well, I was relaxed and enjoying my sandwich. I didn't feel as if I was in a hurry to get home. I was now on the return lap with only about twelve miles to go, so there was no need to think of camping anywhere for the night. The only real threat to the spirit of my tootle now was that I might be tempted to speed up and reach the warmth of my own living room more quickly. There were a few steep hills in front of me and it is hard to climb nonchalantly.

No tootler can be blamed for puffing up a hill. But the proper demeanour for a casual excursion requires that the descent on the other side be enjoyed as a gentle roll. So long as pride in physical achievement doesn't overwhelm the prospect of enjoying the view and the soft sounds of the countryside; so long as you're still noticing things and even chatting away to yourself, wondering why there are so many evangelical churches in Carryduff, for instance, then you're still tootling. But just once succumb to the thrill of speed or the frustration that makes you want to press on and puff harder, and this is no longer a tootle but a race or an ordeal.

At the Carryduff roundabout I have many times before felt the relief that my journey was almost over and I have clunked up the gears to fly down the hill, feeling more as if I was moving through wind than over land, exhilarated, looking forward to a pint or a bath. But this time I held my nerve. I let the bicycle carry me and did not urge it much beyond the speed my own momentum gave it. I tootled. Not perfectly, not all the way to the front door; not absorbing all the sights and smells – who'd want to? – but more than I had before.

I was getting better at this.

Just three months after I'd bought my bike I was rebuking myself for how little cycling I was doing. I had had a bad lingering cold. The June and July weather had been execrable. But I had also been relying too heavily on weather forecasts and I realised that when the weather girls had said there would be showers there were often long unbroken hours of sunshine, time lost to me because I had been too cautious.

Then came a summer Sunday that was perfect. It was dry and bright and more, there was hardly a breeze. But now my habit of procrastination had settled deep in me. There were so many other things to do. It was nice to sit in a deckchair in the garden and read. So, like a recuperating patient who must take things easy, I took the bike into the park before breakfast. I had not seen the park at this time on a Sunday morning before. It was the doggy hour. Dogs, like the rest of us, void their bowels in the morning and there were dozens there, escorted by patient owners with plastic bags in their hands. I made several circuits and tested myself to see how much more relaxed I was on a bike since I had resumed cycling.

O'Brien's theory that we merge with our bikes was inspired apparently by the vision of how the bike will prop against a wall or stand at the kerb supported by one lowered pedal, much as some countrymen will stand and cogitate, one foot on the pavement, the other on the road. But there are many ways in which the growing acquaintance of a rider with a bike is expressed in the physical ease with which they interact with each other. The most obvious example of this is in how a relaxed cyclist may pedal forward with no hands on the handlebars, perhaps even zipping up a jacket or letting the arms dangle to the side in an exaggerated affectation of indifference. I had been able to do this in my thirties but my recent efforts to trust the bike to balance itself had been tentative and wary. I had been riding with one hand easily enough but occasionally only lifting the left a few inches and then grabbing the handlebar again in a panic at the first wobble.

That morning in the park I tried more conscientiously to cycle hands-free and transferred the work of balancing from my arms to my hips, my hands raised from the front, twitching anxiously but well clear. And it worked.

And there is another way in which a bike and its owner will cooperate but which this bike would not oblige in. A real cyclist can walk beside his machine with a hand resting on the saddle and the bike will stay beside him in a straight line, the front wheel obeying no physical law but staying straight only because the whole bike has become an expression of the will of the rider. My bike wouldn't do that. Some people can give their bike a little shove and propel it forward in a straight line. This bike would have been easier to guide along the garden path between the flowering pots if it had had such discipline. It didn't. It wasn't sufficiently well trained to adapt to my will.

Yet I was finding that old habits in the handling of a bike were coming back to me. For instance, I have a way of propping my foot on the pedal while the bar of the bike rests against my knee, snugly under the kneecap, pressing the tendon. This allows me to bend over and tuck my trouser-cuff into my sock, without using my hands to hold the bike. That's all. But I might otherwise need to lean the bike against a wall and find some other step to raise my foot on to. We could coordinate in elementary symbiosis. I propped the bike and the bike propped me. Nothing to it really.

There is a way of propping yourself against a bike, using it almost like a shooting stick. Tilted, it should be easy to rest your bum on the bar. You see cyclists gathered talking to each other like that. Another way is to lean into the bike, the upper part of your own body over the handlebars, as if it is necessary to caress it, reassure it that you haven't taken your mind off it. Gradually my body disclosed its memory of how I did things that I hadn't done for years. So, in the park, sensible people walking their dogs will have watched this man of sixty trying to ride a bike like a teenager or a Tour de France champion and will have thought him both ungainly and immature. They will have wondered why he hadn't the simple good sense to ride a bicycle properly and not jeopardise his ageing bones. Is it not enough to be on your own two wheels but that you have to be acting the lig?

The most challenging part of fusing with a bicycle for me was getting used to the cleats, yet nothing else advances that relationship so fast as falling off. That afternoon I got kitted out properly in my padded shorts and shoes and set out across town to join the Comber Greenway, past the backs of houses and out into the countryside.

I managed well. I didn't fall over. I gave myself time to get out of the cleats before stopping but I saw that other cyclists would stay in them and balance on the stationary bike or prop themselves against a wall. I had come to appreciate the benefit of the cleats more than I feared they would trap me.

At Comber, I rode out towards Castle Espie and Nendrum, following the route of the map published by the sustainable transport charity, Sustrans, founded to encourage us all to get out into the open air without burning petrol. The road to Nendrum hops across islands on Strangford Lough via little adjoining causeways, past stern *Private* signs, and forks in the road several times until at Nendrum Fort both paths reject you: one leads on to private land and the other into a golf course.

From there I retraced the route back to the mainland for a view from another angle of the land the rich preserve for themselves. I don't know who these people are or how they would respond to a casual caller, perhaps looking for a top-up of his water bottle, and I suppose they need their private signs or cars and bikes would be frequently getting lost in their little woodland estates, mistaking their long driveways for public roads. But I wonder if they enjoy proclaiming their ownership of patches of nature in this way, or if, when they drive out into the world the rest of us use too they are embarrassed at having to advertise their separateness.

But they have spent their money well on access to the view of the evening sun on a tide-settled Strangford Lough and the comfort of their conservatories to protect them from the rain that a passing cyclist on the road must struggle against for another two hours before he is home.

10 The dogs of Tyrone

I often drive to Strabane where Maureen grew up and where her mother still lives, but for me the attraction in Tyrone is that it borders Donegal; it's a good stopping off place for a trip to the far west and the beach. Now I could strap the bike to the car and try it out on the mountainy roads close to the border. Maureen's brother Colin rides with a local team, and he appraised my Panorama with an expert's eye. 'Grand bike,' he said. 'You'll have no trouble doing a hundred miles on that.'

The Sustrans routes around the Sperrins and west Tyrone are short, mostly circuits of about thirty miles. Their challenge is in gradient. I grabbed a couple of hours on a midweek afternoon in Strabane to try a circuit that would take me from Sion Mills through Castlederg and home by Newtownstewart. It seems sometimes that the less time I have for a trip the longer it takes me to prepare for it. Procrastination had already crashed into lunchtime – so I had to eat before I left. Which was a time-consuming nuisance, even though I had prepared the crassest doorstep cheese sandwich posible, the sort Maureen would want to redeem with mayonnaise and rocket salad if she saw it. And I had to change clothes and in the flap and frenzy even this was complicated. Was it safe to walk across the kitchen floor in shoes with metal cleats under them?

But it was a nice day, slightly overcast with no serious threat of rain. I cycled along the Strabane bypass on a curiously pleasant incline, then to the roundabout on the Melmount Road and right towards Sion Mills. I had maps from Sustrans but these were not as detailed as I needed them to be so I soon lost my way. I didn't find any cycle route sign in Sion Mills, though I'm sure there is one there, but turned right up towards the Glebe to find the hill road to Castlederg.

At the top of the hill I turned left. I should have seen that the map actually indicates a short detour to the right. But I was at least now on a lonely country road and high in the hills, with barley fields and pasture around me and little sound but birdsong and barking dogs. Dogs seem to me to be generally primed for hostility to cyclists in this part of the country. Perhaps they sense that we are an affront to nature. Any moving animal, experience tells them, should bob a little as it moves. The usual exceptions are stalking hunters, like big cats, much to be feared.

And soon the road was winding downhill, which should have been a warning to me. If I was coming off the mountain so soon, I should have known that I wasn't going in the right direction. I could have kicked myself when I saw that my soaring and banking down the stretched-out helter-skelter had only taken me back on to the A5 from Strabane to Newtownstewart. I was further along the road I had just turned off. Properly, I should then have gone back up that hill to find the turn I had missed but the hills ahead always seem a more acceptable challenge for your not knowing them yet. Going back would have felt too much like paying for pleasure I had already had.

So I took another look at the map. I found I could go down the A5 for a mile and pick up the route again in the other direction. So that's what I did. I turned off the main road at Victoria Bridge and then toiled up another hill. There I looked for the road that would take me to Newtownstewart. Again I couldn't find a route sign and tried one path promisingly skirting the river only to meet locked gates crossing it after the first bend. Further along there was a steep narrow road to my right, signposted to the town. I had reconciled myself to there being a lot of climbing on this route but I was coming to understand how cycling illustrates the law of karma. The world, I reckon, averages out as smooth, so ride for long enough and you will go downhill as much as up, and every struggle will be rewarded with a freewheeling thrill. Try to live a cycling life without paying your dues in breathless struggle and sore legs, and you will always be denied your comfort when you are most hoping to indulge it. Just like life.

This was a lovely road, high over the whole county and with almost no traffic on it. It was only wide enough for one car anyway and the hump along the middle was thick in small gravelly stones that, on a busy road, would have been brushed away by a car wheels. I met one tractor and, further on, a farmer in blue overalls walking his dog. He was wearing incongruously stylish sunglasses.

And I saw the cycle route sign that confirmed I was going the right way, if in the opposite direction to the one I had started out in. At Newtownstewart, the signs guided me to an underpass and into the town. Here the route diverged from another to the east of it with which it had shared the mountain road from Douglas Bridge. I could go left to Gortin Glen Forest or right to Harry Avery's Castle, the Baronscourt estate and Castlederg but I hadn't left myself enough time for the whole route. I took the long climb to the castle in my lowest gear most of the way, riling the dogs at every gate, some of them yelping in high pitch, others with the more worrying deep bass profundo growls of dangerous beasts.

At the very top of the hill I was confronted with a large beefy reddish-brown mastiff, a dog that shifted on its legs to manage its weight and wavered on the impulse to lunge. There was slobbery grime on the big teeth that fronted his jaw, a box large enough to grind hefty chunks of torn flesh in. This was one of nature's thugs. I stood down off my bike to watch this ugly threat, expecting him to charge at me if I moved but otherwise to rage a while and then get bored. I thought I could trust that he was stupid. But I miscalculated when I chanced getting back on the bike and he rushed at me. Then he paused and thought again when I stood firmly and waited for him. I've little doubt he would have taken my leg if I had run.

This could have continued for an hour but a van came up the hill and as it passed between us, I stepped on to my pedal and rolled back the way I had come up, leaving the dog perhaps regretting that he hadn't attacked more confidently and resolving to pounce without reserve the next time a brazen cyclist chanced a confrontation.

I was left wondering if there was some weapon I could legally carry that would empower me to kill or at least disable a dog like this in self-defence. Once, after being mugged in a Paris metro, I equipped myself with a small weapon that might pass for an innocent artefact and carried it for months until my anxiety about strangers on escalators left me. Now, as I cycled away, I was mentally contriving similar plans to arm myself with household items that a man might plausibly explain carrying about him but which, applied imaginatively and at speed, might blind, cripple or eviscerate a large beast.

Given the little time left, I took the A5 at Newtownstewart back towards Strabane. This was mostly a safe and uneventful ride on a level road. The nearest thing to an adventure was my having to stop with the traffic while a farmer escorted his muck-dripping cattle across the road. Then just after Victoria Bridge I found the hill I had come down on my early exhilarating wrong turn. I had a notion that I could take that road now and recompense for my folly and bad map-reading, and for the presumption that I could get to where I was going more by rolling downhill more than puffing uphill. I climbed that winding road back up to the Glebe then rattled downhill into

Clady where I could take the Urney Road back to Strabane. This was an ascent in giant steps, one wobbly exertion after another with the legs weakening further on every turn of the pedal so that in time it seemed a marvel that there was any work left in them.

The nettles growing out of the hedgerows presented another hazard, brushing the back of my hand as I passed, a particular danger when I was inching as close to the verge as I could to make space for unthinking drivers. I stopped at a barley field to photograph the wet stalks in the evening light and, clumsily wrenching myself from my cleats, bounced off the saddle with my whole weight descending abruptly on the bar. The pain such a blow evokes is like the sensation of having a cattle prod touch a nerve or funny-bone deep inside the abdomen. It is the sort of pain that the conscious mind usually interprets as terminally damaging. But I reassured myself that a lifetime of bad karma was probably expended in that one shocking moment.

The descent into Clady could not have been more thrilling on a hang-glider. Here I had the value of my robust and heavy touring bike, stable in its own momentum, crashing through the wind that opposed me, the road clear of all danger in front of me, freeing me to go faster and faster. I had earned it.

When I got home I felt I was ready to tackle a really long run. So I chose the eighty-two-mile Sustrans route round Strangford Lough in the hope that I would get home that night. Mercifully, Irish summer days are long. Like most runs out of Belfast, the route started with city streets and then the Comber Greenway. From the Greenway, the road diverges from the direct road to Killinchy and Killyleagh, and leads on to islands in the lough, by Sketrick Island and over steep drumlins, where the tarmac has grassy lines along the middle of it.

While I stayed with this mapped route I saw almost no traffic. It is still possible to cycle through rural Ireland in the same kind of peace and freedom that you would have enjoyed in the 1950s. I might have been touring the Ireland of my childhood, apart from the evident prosperity of the households I passed, many of them up for sale. In the 1950s only the poor would have lived here, small farmers and farm labourers; now it was mainly the rich though they were leaving now, the economic collapse having left them without enough money to get by on. These people had tamed and manicured the countryside then lost it.

An immediate contrast with cycling in similar hills around Strabane a few days earlier was that here there was no bother from dogs. I don't know how to explain that. Passing one garden gate, though, a couple of large frantic geese harried me.

Robert Penn describes a kind of self-sufficiency in which the cyclist travels only with a credit card. This wouldn't work in the village shops of County Down. I had been careless and had come away with only a bottle of water, a banana and an apple. In Killyleagh I was aching with hunger but I had not the will to break my momentum and stop to eat something. This was a mistake I was making over and over again when cycling distances. I took the direct route to Downpatrick, though Sustrans would have had me turn off, and I found a restaurant just after the turn to Strangford. I bolted the bike to the stay of a telegraph pole and hobbled into the long dark bar where a young man offered me a menu.

'What's your cod like?'

'Lovely,' he said.

So I ordered cod with creamed potatoes and sat down and browsed my e-mail on my phone. I don't think it was anything I did but suddenly the lights ticked off and a continuous whine shrilled from something, probably an alarm. So much for my cod. Would I like a sandwich?

But when I got back on the bike I was a little unsteady

on sore legs. I even set out in the wrong direction, towards Saul and the massive statue of Saint Patrick. Past the highest point on the road I saw another cyclist climbing back on to the saddle after the ascent on foot and pushing from the other side. The road down was long and steep. I wondered if I would have made it up there myself.

My thighs were beginning to groan more importunately and make me doubt that they would function much further. The road from here to Strangford was reasonably forgiving. I wasn't tired in the way I would have been if I had driven too far in the car. Nor was I breathless or weary. I was in no danger of dozing off. I simply felt that I had come out with the wrong legs and they had stopped working for me. But they were the only pair I had so I tried to assuage them by finding better combinations of gears and effort to suit them, sometimes pushing a little harder to get to Strangford quicker, sometimes going into a very low gear and putting up with the frustration of slow progress, essentially trying to trade with them, to suggest compromises that might elicit a bit more tolerance.

That way, I made it into the town and called on my friend Kevin Og in the newsagent in the square. Kevin was not one of nature's cyclists and I think he was a little surprised to find that I might be. 'Did you cycle all the way from Belfast today?' He was prepared to be amazed at my having done about half of the distance I had covered, which was decent of him. I, however, wanted credit for every mile and hill. He sat me down on a crate and served me tea while I rubbed my legs and showed him on the map where I had been. He would have given me all the chocolate I could have eaten but I thought I should watch my sugar levels. Only now did I notice how far I had diverted from the direct route from Belfast. The Sustrans people had designed a route for the cyclist who likes to meander uphill, who is only going to be bored with level ground and a consistent speed, and who has the physical prowess to enjoy eighty miles of cycling, perhaps broken only by lunch. I was not in that league. I phoned Maureen and told her I might have overdone it. 'Well, could you put the bike on a bus?'

That wasn't what I wanted her to say. The sense of failure and defeat would have been unsustainable. The only alternative to getting home that would concur with my sense of myself as a cowboy or pilgrim would have been to sleep under the stars and continue again in the morning.

When I was picking myself up another cyclist came into the shop. He looked like the real thing in his sleek gear. Cyclists are different from other men in that they will fancy that they look fit and sparky while wearing pads at the crotch that look like hefty nappies.

'Have you come far?'

He guzzled from a bottle and between gulps told me that he had started out from Larne and had been to Newcastle. 'I like, every once in a while, to do a ton in a day.'

He appeared to be mistaking me for someone who shared the same goal in life.

And we rolled down to the ferry together where the conductor gathering fares took us for old mates.

'Two pounds for everything.'

We propped the bikes against the wall of the ferry and my new friend told me he was going to swim this same channel as part of a triathlon.

'You're mad.'

I couldn't conceive of the effort involved in swimming to Portaferry, cycling round the lough and then running ten miles.

'Are you part of a club?'

'No, I ride solo.' He was trying to impress me.

We hovered around each other for a couple of minutes, not sure if we were bonding. I felt I should say at this stage that there was no point in us cycling on together since I would not be able to keep up with him. I told him about my thighs. He said he had been having trouble with his hamstrings and ran a finger along the back of his knee to show me. I wondered if cycling was the perfect cover for gay flirting. In no time at all you are discussing your bodies and your rides.

But he drifted away to the upper deck and I assume he had worked out that I was not a natural partner for him. When we were getting off he had another companion on foot and wheeled his bike by hand to stay side by side with him. They seemed very interested in each other.

From the ferry port I followed the coastal route. Strangford Lough was metallically grey in the evening light. My thighs didn't ache so much now so I felt I might make it home okay. I was twenty-eight miles from my wife and dinner. I took the pace easy and stopped a few times to take photographs of the water and the drumlins and just to listen to the silence threaded with birdsong and stirrings on the lough. If I could suspend any fretting about whether I actually had the strength to get home, I would enjoy this part of the route.

I came out on to the busy main road up the western side of the jug handle of the Ards Peninsula and passed through Kircubbin and Greyabbey. At Greyabbey the pain was beginning to frustrate me. This was where Toby and I had often stopped to eat when we had cycled round the lough in the 1980s. I should have stopped and had a meal but much of the town was decked with flags and there were young men milling about and I didn't feel at home there.

Instead, I stopped by the water's edge a couple of miles further on and rested and rubbed my thighs and phoned Maureen and told her I expected to be home by nine. There were only another 15 miles to go. I was aching badly when I passed Newtownards and took the long hill road out of town. This was horrible now. I couldn't keep my balance well in the lowest gear and kept moving between options on the lower range.

But I did examine my state of mind and body. Why are you doing this? I asked myself. It seemed a fundamentally stupid way to be passing a summer's evening, potentially dangerous too. It was one thing to cycle confidently in traffic with a fit body and alert senses. When my confidence came from a slack-bodied blithe contempt for the moment, I knew I was more likely to misjudge the distance of the car coming from behind. But at least there was a long roll from the top of that hill leaving Newtownards. There I tried to assess what my thighs would most appreciate – the exercise of easy pedalling with the reward of speed or just a rest while I freewheeled. I went for the pedalling to get home quicker.

Passing Stormont I saw another cyclist in front of me. He was pedalling much faster than I was but in the lower gear that carried him along no faster than me. I got quite preoccupied with this, wondering why anyone would cycle in such a way. Were his legs so weak that they couldn't push the pedal firmly yet so nimble that they could spin round the crank? Yet I was so tired now that even he pulled away ahead of me after a mile.

As I got closer to home, I thought the enthusiasm for a rest and a dinner would give me a little spurt towards the end but now my legs were sick of the whole exercise and giving me nothing in return for my demands on them. I doubt if I could have gone any further than I had to. When I got off I found I could hardly walk. I went upstairs for a shower that was painful and slow. I was like a helpless old man standing in the bath, in danger of crumpling to my knees. Dinner was lovely but I didn't have much of an appetite. I had no desire for wine but drank a lot of water. When I began to shiver Maureen wrapped a blanket round me and I curled up on the sofa, beaten and defeated.

I'd cycled much further than I had been able for – about seventy miles – half of that over hilly terrain. But that was the kind of cycling I wanted to be able to achieve without pain and grief. I had learnt a sharp lesson in riding sensibly now. I had the benefit of my new fitness to the extent that I would not be hobbled by aching muscles for days but I really had to discipline myself to eat and rest properly on big trips.

11 A real cyclist again?

One of the biggest challenges for the cyclist is Lough Neagh, slap in the middle of Northern Ireland. Anyone looking at a map, never having been here, would assume that this massive inland lake must be the biggest tourist attraction in the country. In fact, it is barely accessible round most of its perimeter and few tourists go anywhere near it. Sustrans has mapped a route around it and there are organised cycling trips every year but you can go on one of these and see little water.

I felt that it was too much to do on one day, at my level of fitness, so my neighbour Patrick and I planned a trip that would break about half way, in Magherafelt. Patrick was, I guessed, much fitter than me, but he had been good company on an earlier run and if he had been slowing down for me he, at least, didn't make that obvious. Our wives would drive to a guest house there and we'd all have dinner together; the idea being that you can be a cyclist and a civilised person too, blending the rough life on the road that I was trying to recreate with the luxuries Maureen had taught me to enjoy, though – for the sake of my gut – I was indulging them more sparingly now. So, relying on the Sustrans map, Patrick and I set out on a Saturday morning in July along the Lagan towpath. The river was as still as polished metal and the path was cluttered in places by other cyclists and Action Cancer walkers coming the other way from Lisburn.

Patrick was riding a Dawes Galaxy which was more than ten years old. When he first got it he stripped off the mudguards and carrier to make it look more like a racer. Now he had fitted a new rear mudguard but for want of a carrier wore a rucksack on his back. I had my nifty pannier slung to the side behind my saddle.

At first we were both relaxed and cycling smoothly; the danger of being tipped into the river imposed caution on us. We talked about the economy and the great ideas that people we knew had had for making money. We wondered if any big idea like that would one day come to either of us. We passed a swans' nest in long grass by the river's edge, where the cygnets still had grey down. Then we were suddenly in the middle of Lisburn and skirting the Island Arts Centre to pick up the last stretch of riverside path beyond it.

There is a little excitement in reaching a road from a riverside route. The road seems almost to be a river of a different kind, carrying breezes from where it has been and hints of where it will take you. We had no map covering this section but thought we could rely on the Sustrans signs and, sure enough, the first junction was well marked. Then Patrick called to me to stop. He had a puncture in his rear wheel.

We turned into a narrow country road, away from the traffic, and he unclipped the cable from his brakes to ease off the wheel. Between us we were equipped to deal with the problem. I had levers and he had a spare tube. First he pumped up the old tube held in front of him, and turned it and listened for the hiss. Then we checked the tyre itself for a thorn or piece of glass. It seemed clean. But they were old worn tyres.

Another cyclist stopped to offer help, a man of about our own age with greying curly hair and a shiny anorak. 'A mighty shower came down on me in Aghagallon,' he said. We had seen no rain yet. And we talked about where we were going. He said he was an amateur, trying to get his miles up. 'I went out with a club last week and they did 67 miles at 19.1 miles an hour. I was dead at the end of it.'

He was, like me, one of the late returners to cycling but he wasn't intent on being a tootler; he was working to achieve fitness and speed. I try to maintain that cycling doesn't need to be a race against your own physical limits; that we are free to cycle as we walk and not always as we run but this man had found in his return to cycling a reminder of his own weakness and was compelled by the discovery to test himself every time he went out for a ride.

I worried that Patrick was doing the same thing when he overtook me and set the pace towards Moira. I watched his style and saw that it was different from my own. He almost never sat on the saddle or went down into the lower gears. And he sprinted. He would pedal fiercely for a few yards and then roll on the momentum he had created. I did that when I was burnt out at the end of a long trip so I wondered if he was tired now but it was soon obvious that he had much more stamina than I had.

We crossed the motorway bridge and a little further on, at a junction, stopped to ponder which direction we should turn. We propped the bikes and had a sandwich and some cashew nuts on a grass verge and studied the map. I reckoned I knew where we were from the position of the motorway but we could not find the Sustrans sign to confirm that we were even still on the cycle network. This should have been a crossroads, by my calculation, but it was T-junction. 'Maybe there is a left turn a bit further to the right,' said Patrick.

Well, for the map to be accurate, it would have to have been only yards away. We cycled a mile up the road and found a left turning but it was narrow and there was still no sign for cyclists. Patrick suggested we go back the way we had come and see if there was a turning to the south of the confusing junction. The rain was coming on now, gently at first but building. We followed the road back to where we had been and beyond and hit the A1 from Lisburn to Hillsborough, which told us, in effect, that we had travelled no real distance at all. But at least it gave us our bearings.

We'd turn around again and stay on this road, and we would reach Moira and pick up the route. The rain was heavy now. I had a little jacket that was as fine as rice paper but the man in Bike Dock had assured me it was waterproof, unlikely as that seemed. I could feel the cold of the rain on it pressed against my skin by the breeze and I could feel my own sweat dampening my vest and jersey underneath. The miracle technology that prevented osmosis between these fluids began to seem almost superfluous, an unnecessary marvel given that there was no chance of me actually staying dry. Then the rain got heavier. The water began to streak off the wondrous fabric. I was getting the value of it now. But the water ran off my jacket on to my legs, which had only cotton to protect them.

'Uh oh!'

I stopped

'Another puncture,' said Patrick, clearly humiliated now by his old bike. We turned into another country lane, the access road to a farm. This time we would need to repair the puncture itself and not just replace the tube. But we were both wondering if there was any point. If Patrick was going to get a flat every five or six miles, then we would have to abort this trip or find a bicycle shop where he could get new tyres.

He got the tube out and pumped it up to listen for the hiss again. I had patches and he took one and pressed it on but there was no way to keep the repair dry in the rain and it didn't take. Then he used his own patches with glue and inflated the tube and it seemed to hold until we got it on to the wheel and the tyre half fitted. Then he thought he heard the hiss again. He took the tube out and we stood in the rain, learning admirable things about each other's temperament, listening to the rubber for another missed puncture or seepage of air from under the patch. 'You know, Patrick, you can buy puncture resistant tyres. Or you can get gel to pump into them that seals the puncture before you know you've got it.'

We couldn't find the hiss. I squeezed the tube like I was testing a sausage for freshness, for texture and resilience. It was firm. 'No problem there,' I said. We were now so wet it hardly seemed to matter how heavy the rain got, but back on the road and moving, it felt heavier and colder still and my glasses blurred over. But we found the network again just short of Moira and would be fine now until the next time we got lost – or until the next puncture.

The road west from Moira was a little hilly and large puddles had gathered in the dips but Patrick's rear tyre held up and we put on a bit more speed. We seemed to be going in the right direction. We came out into an urban area. The logical thing to have asked ourselves – or somebody – would have been, 'what town is this?' But there was a cycle network sign on a wall facing us and even a group of cyclists tearing past it towards the north.

I checked the map. I reasoned that if I traced our route so far to the point where it met the numbered route that now crossed our paths, I would locate our actual position. Logical? I thought so. I didn't know it yet but I was out by miles. But we studied the map between showers and trusted we knew where we were. We could see that there were a couple of meanders towards the shore of the lough that we could short-circuit to save time. But we wouldn't find them because we weren't where we thought we were.

For now we decided to follow the route of the Sustrans route number 94 round the lough. A problem was that some of the signs were difficult to find. Some were unclear about whether they would take us round the lough to the west or to the east, for it is the same number on the route each way. Sustrans had erected these on available posts positioned for other purposes so they weren't always best placed to be seen in time. Patrick and I had discussed which direction to take around the lough. I had been in favour of going anticlockwise. One advantage would be that every turning would be a left turning. He favoured cycling clockwise, leaving us an easy return to Belfast next day, when we would be knackered. That's what we settled on.

'At last the lough,' said Patrick. It was grim and overcast and raining lightly and the whole of Lough Neagh was spread out beside us like a puddle from a million years of weather like this. 'It's on the wrong side,' I said. We stopped to try and read the map but I couldn't see it without my glasses and I couldn't see through them because they were wet. Logically we should turn around now and cycle till we found the last Sustrans sign that we had clearly missed. That's what we did but we nearly missed it again, two wet miles later. The water running off my high-tech jacket had drenched my trouser legs. The cotton would not have been wetter if I had waded through a river.

Well, I thought, ask yourself now if this is worth the trouble. Interrogate your inner being and see if there is any fragment of contentment at the heart of confusion and discomfort. Ask why you're doing this. And I did, in the spirit of the professional observer and note-taker. And what I found was that I was entirely and illogically at peace with myself, aching, wet and tired, and as happy as a child in a mud bath.

The missed turning, when we found it, sent us along a gravelly riverside path and down a mucky lane where we met a man on a quad bike who was a bit of a muck baby himself, by the look of him. He was wet and amiable. We asked about the route and he knew all the details of it well. Apparently local farmers around the lough are acquainted with the network and well used to advising lost cyclists. 'But how will you get over the Bann?' he said. 'You will have to go into Portadown.' We were supposed to be out enjoying a ride in the country, but to stay on the route we would have to go right into a busy town centre. We'd been gambling on finding a bridge over the Bann that would spare us that. We actually went through two towns, for we took in Lurgan as well, both on the busiest day of trading, when traffic was heavy and hazardous and we were as wet as if we had been hosed down. And unable to see clearly through wet glasses. These were things I would have to ask about; lenses that stay clear in heavy rain and waterproof leggings.

The first woman we asked for directions to Portadown from Lurgan didn't know where Portadown was. The second said it was six miles away. 'You go round the church and get into the left lane.' Which shows you the differing levels of awareness that can be found between different members of the same population in close proximity to each other. Now, instead of tootling along the lough shore, we were belting round the roundabouts of the open country called Craigavon, where a city had been planned but not built.

In time we converged with cars coming off the motorway into Portadown. When the two lanes of traffic stalled, I watched Patrick make his way ahead between them, so I followed him, tentatively at first and then more confident that drivers would avoid hitting me if they could. There had been an accident and the police were guiding cars around it. We went into the complex junction that separates traffic flows for Armagh and Dungannon and then took the hill on the A6 back towards the lough.

While we had our minds on the danger posed by the traffic, the rain stopped. Within two miles my clothes were dry again, except for my socks, and we stopped at a garage for another bite, to buy fresh water and to phone ahead. I called the guesthouse in Magherafelt and asked them to change our dinner booking. Had the wives arrived yet? No.

I phoned Maureen and told her that we were coming out of Portadown. The image of us cycling through the town centre in the rain alarmed her but I told we were all right. And we were, except that I was fading now. We had done fifty miles, according to Patrick's handlebar computer, only to reach a town that was thirty-five miles from home, and we still had not seen much of the beautiful Lough Neagh that had drawn us out of our beds that morning. 'We would have been better putting the bikes on the train and starting from here,' said Patrick. We would.

But the sun was out now and it was open if undulating countryside, and we were cycling among barley fields and birdsong. I was finding some of the hills tough. Another few miles took us back to the M1 which we had crossed so often that it seemed to be taunting us with a reminder that sane people travel by car, get there faster and arrive dry.

We reached Maghery and the lough. It was a glorious and heartening evening. One could not imagine a more golden and beautiful time or place. We rested by the water's edge and watched fishing boats coming in. The clarity of the sound of their engines and the lapping of the water seemed only to accentuate by contrast the peace they meekly disturbed. 'How much further?' Patrick said he'd call his wife at the guesthouse and get her to come and pick us up.

'That's not in the spirit of it.'

But he knew I was even more tired than he was.

We decided to follow the route north and then fork off it into Stewartstown. The land was level for a few miles, over stripped bog, though the tarmac surface of the road was broken in places, as if the soft earth underneath could not support it. There were steep hills before Stewartstown but we felt like heroes having cycled sixty-three miles in awful conditions when we slumped on to benches in the town square and waited for our lift.

We didn't have to wait long. Ann and Maureen arrived in a big car with room for us to squeeze our bikes in if we took off the wheels. I expected they would slag us off for not finishing the journey. They were jubilant to find us safe and told us they thought we were marvellous. Well that's what we thought too. But a husband who is legless from cycling all day is no more fun than one who is legless in any other way. We went out for dinner, the four of us, but I was almost numb with fatigue and little joy to be with. I went to bed doubting that I could finish the journey next day. The car could take us all home if that was what we wanted.

We stayed in a guest house that was like a shrine to poet

Seamus Heaney, in a bedroom with some of his poems framed on the walls. Patrick and Ann got the Longley Room, dedicated to Michael Longley. I had known guest houses before that were hung with pictures of the saints and the Kennedys and preferred this. I woke with aches in my back and my legs stiff, still grim from the intensity of concentration that had kept me on the road, then paused to consider what I really wanted to do now.

I was as surprised at the answer from within as the others would be when I said over breakfast that I was up for finishing the circuit. At least we could go as far as Antrim on the bikes and then strike out from there to Belfast and cut a big corner. Then we could say we had toured the lough, bar the bit from Stewartstown to Magherafelt, which was not even equal to the effort we had taken to reach the lough from Belfast in the first place. It mightn't be the full Sustrans network route but those routes were murder.

Patrick was feasting cheerfully on the big fry. I said, 'You on for it?'

I don't think he had even considered aborting the tour. I could have pleaded the perfectly reasonable excuse that I was older, a man of sixty, legally entitled to travel home free by public transport, but that would not have been in the spirit of a project to prove that an older man can still keep up.

The first part of our return journey took us through a car park and a bit of woodland and then back on to the road. The sun was out but big silvery clouds threatened rain. We cycled north with the lough beside us part of the way, then short circuited again across farmland then east on a narrow road towards Toome.

There we passed a dead fox on the road. Cycling gives you a closer view of the carnage caused by traffic. We had seen dead birds and one badly squashed squirrel. Badgers seemed to be the most common victims. This was the only fox we had seen in this part of the country. Its eyes were open and its expression was dull but placid. There was little sign of damage though the coat was soaked and drab from the rain. A split in that coat exposed the stomach, like a red plastic balloon, just a little deflated. Patrick was amused by my wanting to stop and photograph it.

'People should notice the waste,' I said.

The route took us right into Toome for the only crossing of the Bann, then sharp right and back out of town along walkways and picnic areas by the water's edge. A couple having breakfast together presumably didn't want to be disturbed. From there we went through a little housing estate then south along the shore on narrow roads with fields on both sides. The land here was flat and Patrick seemed as much inclined as I was merely to tootle. We could have shortened this stage by cutting across country, according to the map, but the aches were easing as the muscles warmed up and we relished the whole section, through places with names on the map but little to show but a few houses: Ballynamullan, Ballynaleny, Killyfad, Staffordstown, Leitrim. There was a bit of a climb before Randalstown, to remind us that cycling is supposed to be hard, then a good long roll into the main street where we stopped again.

On my big trek down the west coast in the 1980s I had always stocked up with wholesome food and carried a little cooker, but now you can buy varieties of packed salads, cheeses and sandwiches in any garage. A cultural change since then is that more people eat out, which appears to include eating snacks in the car. I got a little pasta and mixed peppers salad that I expected to eat with my fingers but there was even a plastic fork for me when I took the lid off. The modern world's provisions for office workers skipping lunch are pretty handy for the traveller too.

The route out of Randalstown, as marked on the map, should have taken us due east past Frenchpark but the signs took us to the roundabout on the motorway and the A6 to Antrim. The hard shoulder was marked as a cycle path so we took that instead of looking for the scenic route. It turned into the footpath of the main road and we rolled into Antrim and into the Lough Shore Park where families were out taking the sun and where crazed jet-skiers competed to do more and more dangerous sharp turns and skids. And a little brass band played leisurely jazz numbers.

It surprised me that this was such a pleasant spot, a major attraction only twenty miles from home and yet I had never seen it before. After another scoffing of nuts for more energy we set a steady pace for Templepatrick and for the roundabout splitting traffic for Belfast and traffic for the north, the hairiest part for cyclists. After that we had an easy trail into Belfast.

I had forgotten how used I once was to cycling this road until I found myself almost on automatic, relying on reflexes, coursing down the Antrim Road and round Carlisle Circus and selecting my lane without thinking, crossing Millfield only to almost throw myself off by hitting a kerb at King Street. They must have extended that corner. I steered off the kerb but my left pedal slapped flat on to the kerb stone and scraped it. I seemed about to flap over into the traffic when my balance corrected itself and I was okay.

And then the rain came on, five minutes from home.

It was as if the gods had favoured our efforts by holding back the shower until we were almost finished. And that would have been fair of them, for we had proven ourselves up to the challenge we had set, and more than that, we had enjoyed the free and easy cycling of the second day, exploring new territory and fitting well together. This was more like real cycling, going far, stretching yourself in good company and arriving home fit to do the same again if you have to, not wrecked by the effort.

You haven't really done fifty miles on a bike if the last ten were agony; then you are only cycling on because you have no choice. So that was the day I felt I had finally made it and become a real cyclist again.

12 The Antrim Coast

My earliest childhood memories are of Ballycastle and a little housing estate at the foot of Knocklayde, the hump mountain that my mother said was the home of the bogeyman who would come and get little children who didn't behave. As I recall, the bogeyman inspired more curiosity than fear in me.

My grandparents – on my mother's side – lived in a cottage nearby on Coleraine Road. They had a long garden at the back for growing vegetables, runner beans, sweet peas – and a more awesome space at the front with sculpted bushes whose incongruity impressed me even then. It was at that time that my father lived in Belfast, in digs, while working as a barman in the Distillery Bar on the Grosvenor Road. He travelled up to see us and, presumably, to give my mother her housekeeping money. And because he only came once or twice a week, often on his bike, his presence was always a treat and he sat at the fire and bounced his little boys on his knees.

Ballycastle and the area around it is not conducive to cycling. I go there often and rent the old coastguard's tower. My mother's father, William O'Halloran, was a coastguard from Ballycastle and presumably worked out of that tower and lived for a time in one of the little cottages which flank it. The other cottage on Coleraine Road was part of his retirement package, the long acre at the back measured out as sufficient to feed him. The tower is on a lane off the main coast road out of Ballycastle to the west, a steep hill that rises from the roundabout by the shore. The highlights of that area when I knew it as a child were the jutting of rocky Fair Head into the sea – a child's first thought was of how awful it might be to fall from there – and an old sea mine which had been converted into a collection box and painted red.

'Could it still explode?'

'Well don't go kicking it like that or you might find out.'

Ballycastle has a lot of steep hills. One of them is Clare Street which we walked up to the little primary school run by the nuns of the Cross and Passion, so called I think, because their passion was the cross we had to bear.

In Ballycastle, the butcher Terence Donnelly has decorated his window with the old delivery bike that he used when he was twelve years old to bring parcels of meat to the nuns in the convent or to the Marine Hotel. He was a delivery boy until he was eighteen and the bike was decommissioned in 1976.

That type of bike was a standard of grocers and other shops. It had a big basket at the front over a small wheel and a large stand that propped the front but could be folded back before casting off on to the road again. Terence Donnelly's bike was older than him by one year. When I asked him about it he went looking for the receipt to confirm the price his father had paid for it. He bought it from N. Gillespie of Clare Street, Ballycastle – a shop I must have passed on my way to school. Perhaps the bike was bright and new in the window then. Gillespie was a member of the National Association of Cycle Traders and he described himself as a Cycle and Motorcycle Agent. In those days bikes and motorbikes were thought of as belonging to the one class of product. But his handwriting hasn't lasted as long as his bike and the price has faded. Now the bicycle is repainted to be decorative but the tyres are flat. The old brakes operated on solid bars rather than cables and the bike had no gears at all. It had served a town of steep hills that exact a price for the joy of tootling down them.

The Torr Road that leads out of Ballycastle, round the coast towards Cushendun, has stretches that are so steep that even motorists find them daunting. It is now part of the cycling network but I met no other cyclist on it the day I tried it. Maureen and I had rented the coastguard's tower for two weeks in summer. This was my first visit to the area since I had resumed cycling, so I had strapped the bike to the back of the car anticipating my greatest challenge yet, a punishing road. Children and light cyclists prefer the little road that follows the coast east as far as Marconi's cottage. Marconi is said to have tested the first radio message from there, though a sign erected in the parking space near the cottage says this is disputed. But the history of the house provides an excuse for the only accessible short level route in the area that might allow the tourist to say, 'I have been out on my bike.'

There is a more arduous walk for those who want to make a substantial trip. They can climb Knocklayde. I did it some years ago. I had to give up short of the summit more recently but I am lighter and fitter now and think I'd be fine. Sure, didn't I cycle the Torr Road?

If there is a right way to ride up a steep hill it is to stand and lean over the handlebars and pump the pedals hard, not in a very low gear but in a mid-range gear on a bike like the Panorama. Any weight being lifted should ideally be directly above the force applied to it. If you sit back in the saddle the centre of gravity in your upper body weighs down behind you while your legs are pedalling furiously in the granny gear. But the right way is the hard way. It is right because it is the most efficient expenditure of effort for a result, but if the required thrust just isn't available to you – if your legs are not strong enough – then you must sit back and try the low gear and go slower and feel heavier – you are effectively dragging your own body slowly up behind you.

It was the Torr Road that showed me that I was not strong

enough to cycle properly. The best preparation for those hills would be the hardening of the thighs. Riding as I ride feels wimpish and foolish on such winding gradients. I did it, though, for most of the way. I had to get off and push for about a hundred yards on one horrific ascent, but that is an even more inefficient way to get a bicycle and a human body up a hill.

I started out on the turn-off to Corrymeela. This is a steep ride uphill and back down the other side, returning you to the same road you had left, just a little further along. A practical traveller would not have turned off it in the first place. If you're not actually intending to visit Corrymeela there is only one other logical reason for going up there and that is self-mortification. And you get enough of that when you next turn off the A2 at Hunter's Bar.

This is a beautiful journey. For much of it, the sea is close to your left. The Mull of Kintyre is so close that you can make out houses. On a clear day you can see other islands and mountains beyond. But the local close view is as fascinating. You can see the remnants of old potato rills that line the ditches from a day when every patch of land was hungrily exploited, surviving still because no farmer since has needed that ground for anything. It is all pasture land now but – who knows? – the sheep may even find these rills useful as steps down into the ditches for the juicier grass.

I stopped often, not just to rest, but also to savour the view of the hills around me and the sea below, to monitor the showers of rain drifting across from Scotland. I had left the tower when the sun was bright and the sky clear. I had presumed not to bring my rain gear. Now I wasn't sure I should have left it behind.

The usual reward for struggling up a hill is to be able to rattle down the other side but the descents on the Torr Road are treacherous and winding too, and I found myself twitching the brakes every few yards, especially on corners where the hill steepened sharply on the inside of the curve.

The road surface was beautifully smooth. The texture of the tarmac under your tyre means everything to a cyclist and, if the roads were built by people who love bikes, they would all be as fine as glass. Instead, usually they are so coarse and broken that the rubber hisses against the grain and the whole bike judders. Perhaps the Torr Road, being so close to the sea, does not freeze over and break up on the thaw as often as inland roads. Or perhaps there is some official with responsibility for transport who rides a bike and has reasoned that this road is challenge enough already.

There were a few motorcyclists out that day. I suspect they love the turns and dives on this road, though some had stopped to deal with a technical problem; nothing I could have helped with, I'm sure. But I wondered what they, who spend thousands on huge machines and encase themselves in heavy leather, must think of the simple cyclist who proceeds under his or her own power and lets the wind in round the legs and armpits. I think they should feel a rebuke implied by the self-sufficiency of the cyclist. Men of my age can keep their paunches and ride a motorbike so long as they are just nimble enough to get a leg over it. Yet I suppose they travel like this to swagger and proclaim their manhood. But how does the thrust and surge of an engine underneath you make a clearer statement about your actual virility than would your own physical exertion on a push bike? But I'm impressed by the speed and grace, perhaps also by the cheek, of their riding on the best they can purchase, on metal and carbon fuel. They seem to be proclaiming their success in having acquired a machine that absolves them of effort. They're saying 'Aren't I lucky? – not like that poor bugger on his bicycle puffing hard enough to give himself a heart attack or bust a gut.'

The motorcycle seems to declare wealth and ease, the freedom to enjoy an adventure without exertion because you have already paid for it with hard-earned money. We have our motorcycling heroes and they die for their sport, which few cyclists do, so it must be very important to them. Like golf, however, it seems to be a sport you can excel in and keep your paunch.

After about a dozen miles and closer to Cushendun, the hills were smaller and occasionally the speed I gathered coming down one was enough to carry me up the next. At this stage, the view of the sea opened up right in front of me, pewter and dappled, like a rough grey desert stretching to Scotland. I think I made out the Isle of Man. I had a sense of clinging to the edge of a steep landmass in a world that was predominantly water.

When you linger like this on the side of a mountain, looking down at the sea, as an outsider with a mental map that includes most of Ireland, you compare the crags and fields with others that you know in Donegal or Kerry. But then you pause to wonder about the scope of the people who lived here in the past. You can see by the remnants of hungry tillage that they clung to unforgiving slopes for sustenance. Yet they will have known the sea and its vast horizon every day. And when they moved, if they moved at all, it was over water more easily than over land. They are more likely to have known the coastal fringes of Scotland and the north of England and the islands than the territory that is now Ballymena or Monaghan. So if they had a notional home in their minds, with parameters beyond the fields they worked, it is more likely to have been water bounded by coasts than land bounded by sea.

When I lived some years ago in Heysham, where the ferry went, I walked often along the beach to the Barrows, the site of monastic graves on a rocky outcrop. This had been a site dedicated to Saint Patrick and it is one of several on the coast and islands of Britain. It is as Irish as Saul or Croagh Patrick. It just happens to be in England.

Now, below me, was the little crescent beach like the only small cleft in which human habitation could survive between the waves and the shadowy hills, and a few white buildings clustered round it. The town itself seemed incongruously tame once I was off the mountain, having forgotten how hard won its placement there was, though the conversation in the supermarket was biblical. A man was telling a friend how he tried to dissuade his son from going to a certain nightclub.

'I tell him the Lord destroyed Sodom and Gomorrah for that sin, but he won't listen.'

And I wondered if, living among these hills, it might be easy to succumb to the illusion that you live in geological time, in which vast swathes of history and spiritual concerns are foremost. Of course, in reality, the fields there are as tempered by time as the main street.

The long slow haul out of Cushendun to join the A2 was almost a relief from the steep climbs of the Torr Road, though it sapped the energies. At the top, I met six Belfast girls resting in a field by their backpacks. 'Doing the Duke of Ed?'

'Aye, we're only taking a break,' said one of them, as if she felt it was important to provide an excuse for inaction.

'Good on you.'

I passed Loughareema, the vanishing lake. My father told me about this lake when we were young, and it seemed a great mystery that water could disappear and return. There is probably no mystery to it at all. The rain-swollen streams gather on a high bog but have the whole mountain to drain out on to. Or maybe it is the fairies.

The A2 follows the karmic law better than the Torr Road and a long struggle to the top of the hill is rewarded with an equally long roll down the other side. I was going so fast that the wind got into my jacket billowing out the fabric to strain the zip, slide it down to the catch and create a parachute around me. Or was that the fairies again?

Passing the golf course in Ballycastle, a golf ball bounced on the road in front of me. No harm. I wondered for a moment if courtesy required me to stop and throw it back on to the green then decided to let the golfer take care of it himself.

The town looked happy and bright. The hill up to the coastguard's tower was as steep as the others I had taken and I challenged myself to ride up it standing on the pedals. I had enough puff and muscle. I had only to get halfway up anyway. And the nearest I came to an accident was then, when I ran out of momentum still locked into my cleats. I saw the moment coming when I was losing the chance to pause and unclip. My only opportunity would be when I was either falling over or rolling backwards. The legs gave up: the bike stopped. What do real cyclists do now? I wondered. Would I keel to the left or to the right? The right. Then a ripple of panic down my leg got my foot out just in time. To have gone so far and fallen over at the front door would have stripped me of my victory. That reflex saved my hip, my bare arm, my shoulder – and my dignity.

And then suddenly I started to take a downer on cycling. I had chosen to ride round Strangford Lough again on a sunny day in September. I'd woken up to sunlight and a whole free day. I should have set off early and not bothered checking emails or Facebook, for just dealing with a few queries took time, enough time for a little cloud cover to gather. I joked in my Facebook status that I was getting my gel pants on in anticipation of a good ride, and even before I was properly changed the comments were coming in and I was tempted to read them and respond.

When I got away from the computer, the wind was stronger than I'd expected but I was soon through the city traffic and on to the Comber Greenway where the dog walkers still didn't bother with poop bags and some of them had nasty-looking beasts, not even on a lead. At the end of the path I was tempted to just turn back, not because I was tired but because I was bored. I was distracted from cycling by thoughts of the other things I could be doing, not just work. I took and returned calls in a field, sheltering from the traffic noise behind a high hedge. Perhaps I should have had a tablet computer with me. I read my emails on my phone but could not manage long replies on it. I checked up on the witticisms inspired by my Facebook reference to gel pants. I managed to write a little update. My gel pants were not as comfortable as I needed them to be but no amount of readjustment seemed to effect the arrangement I needed. I summed up that dilemma as distinctly as I could for my Facebook friends, a tad bawdily too.

The other problem was that I had chosen the less scenic route around the lough. The cycle network takes you meandering along the water's edge, up and down hills. The last time I had tried that I had been exhausted by Strangford and in agony before I got home. This time I rode through Lisbane and Killyleagh. The roads were more direct but drab too. I was tempted to stop for lunch at Balloo. If I had done that I would probably just have turned for home afterwards. But the smell of food from the restaurant – yummy. Instead I had a Snickers at a garage and ploughed on.

I was beginning to ache on the road towards Castleward and Strangford but worse, to my mind, was an annoying sense that this was all a pointless diversion from my real life. It seemed a dutiful struggle; there was no pleasure in it. Why was I thirty miles from my computer? What was I getting out of this? The surroundings were lovely but I could have come and looked at the fields in my car and then gone home to do some work. Well it was all great exercise. Maybe, but no one goes to a gym and sits for three, four or five hours on the cycling machine. I was supposed to be tootling and enjoying nature, whistling to myself in perfect contentment, on the cusp of autumn, enjoying restored health without a care in the world. But I did have cares and cycling was not solving them.

At Strangford I stopped to see Kevin Og at the shop. He invited me to the house for a cup of tea but I said I needed nutrition and suggested we go across to the Cuan, a bar restaurant. He ordered his pint of cider and my water and we discussed the menu. I fancied the seafood crêpe. We talked about life and the summer and how the world was treating us. When my crêpe arrived, Kevin, a man with experience of eating heavily, said, 'Are you not afraid that will weigh heavily on you with thirty miles to go on the bike still?'

I hadn't thought about that.

'Maybe I shouldn't have said that,' he said with a big grin. 'You'll only worry now.'

But we gave each other a manly hug in the square and I got back on the bike and rolled down to the ferry where, on reflection, I decided that my crêpe was both heavy and restless. I managed the coast road out of Portaferry without this turbulence turning into desperation, yet every time I passed a farm gate I offered myself the option of deferring till the next one the decision to stop and find a quiet corner of a hedgerow and be as natural as a man can be. One concern was that even on a rolling hill, without a sound but the birds, a farm boy might emerge from behind a hay bale. Or those boats on the lough might be full of people scanning the fields with their binoculars.

In time my gut learned to be patient and settled itself, just like the bits in the gel pants that had pinched and ached till my mind drifted away from them. I knew from before that the road out of Newtownards is horrific, a long steep hill, but on the last occasion I had hurt so much in my thighs that the struggle was intermittent and agonising. The reward had been a sense of achievement, survival beyond inconceivable extremity. This time I was fitter and it was merely tedious. The only reward was that I was closer to home, but I could have been closer still if I had not bothered coming out on the bike at all.

So why had I? Months earlier, when I had turned sixty, it had seemed important and potentially exciting to prove that I could cycle the way I had done at thirty. Now I was doing that. Grand. But perhaps I hadn't properly asked myself why I had stopped cycling in my thirties. I had assumed that it was just that I had lost contact with Toby and a routine with him. Then I had got busier in my work and used a car more. Then I had got fat. Well now I wasn't fat any more and I was able to cycle again, but I still had the other deterrents in my life. I had work and a marriage. There would always be something more important to do than traipsing along some country road for hours on end. And I didn't have a social structure around me of other cyclists who'd turn up on my doorstep and say, 'Are you coming out on the bike?'

I could understand now why cyclists devote themselves to more than the pleasure of tootling. Tootling is something you can only enjoy when you have no targets to meet, no other claim on your time, nothing on your mind that can't just be wished away. Tootling on your bike is never more urgent than pottering about the garden or soaking in a bath. The joy is in being free to do it. When you're that free, it hardly matters what you do.

When I spent afternoons and evenings cycling with Toby years ago my girlfriend, Celine, lived in Switzerland so she took up no time at all, really. Indeed, maybe I was busting a gut on the roads round Strangford Lough back then just to keep my mind off the sexlessness of my life. Now I'm married.

Why have I not been cycling for most of the last twenty years? Well, partly because I have been sharing my life with another person who does not cycle much. Maureen sits very nicely on a bike. She likes to go out for a wee ride the odd time. We took the bikes on the car to Donegal and caroused around Rossnowlagh on them. She said: 'I don't mind going for a cycle ride, so long as I know that there is a cappuccino at the end of it.'

What she really meant was that she didn't mind cycling to the nearest available cappuccino, so long as she could then sit down and enjoy it and read the *Irish Times*. On the beach we slalomed round the dead jellyfish, seeing that other cyclists before us had ridden right over some of them, risking the skid.

She got her coffee at a restaurant overlooking Creevy Pier and the astonishing sweep of Donegal Bay. A lone fisherman was dipping his line for mackerel into the edge of the still grey sea fringed by distant hazy blue mountains. In the restaurant, the incessant perky pop music seemed to declare that the proprietors were oblivious to the placid grandeur. On the way back I was able to synchronise my pace with Maureen's and work out that her lowest gear was equivalent to my own middle one and that I could go down a lot further. And her saddle was too low. Yet even with the struggle her enthusiasm seemed to be growing, perhaps in anticipation of the next cappuccino. There was still no way I was going to persuade her to join me on a fifty-mile excursion which would guarantee we would suffer afterwards.

I wonder why cyclists and sports people generally work for exhaustion. Maybe part of the attraction is a little despicable, a bit like the drug-user's need to burn up time that would otherwise be too painful to endure. At the end of a long struggle, when you are lying stretched out and groaning as your muscles try to unwind, you have the perfect excuse for letting someone else make the tea or for not going upstairs to your study right now and filling in your tax return. Maybe we invent these challenges for ourselves to make up for the lack of heart for real endeavour; maybe we push and pant to help us imagine we are contesting the real challenges of life when we are doing no such thing; perhaps we carry in our genes the expectation that we will fight and the reward programmed into us is sensuous exhaustion.

A cyclist may indulge the pain of sore muscle the way a certain kind of narcissistic alcoholic relishes his hangover. The groaning body is somehow recognised by our minds as proof of achievement, but maybe cycling or running or doing push-ups is the grasp for a phoney high, more like self-indulgence than work. Go out and batter yourself against the hills and you may come home feeling like a hunter or warrior but you cannot expect your wife to share in your sense of heroism when there is no material advance in your collective domestic comfort to show for it.

'And don't leave your gel pants lying on the bathroom floor!'

And sometimes she'll say. 'If it's exercise you want, go and hoover the stairs.'

But we cycle because we enjoy it. Of course it is good to be fit, isn't it? And if fitness is only a by-product of cycling then there must be some other value in spending hours on a bike travelling to somewhere you don't need to go. I think the paradox is that cycling is leisure and yet it is exhausting. For most people, leisure is what you take when you are tired already. I had thought I would reach a level of fitness that would make long-distance cycling easy and enjoyable. This had not happened. There would always be pain. So there had to be another reason to bother. Other cyclists created those reasons with time trials, races, group excursions. They set themselves targets and these served to keep them lashed to the routine.

I had made a breakthrough in finding freedom on a bike but I didn't really know yet what to use that freedom for. But if I was to retract a little, stop exerting myself and just integrate the bike into my life as a vehicle for getting about the city or dawdling along the river, then I might become one of those cyclists whose machine is as ordinary and uninteresting to them as their shoes. You might like your shoes when you buy them, but you don't want them taking up any of your attention while you are going about in them. You don't go out for a walk to indulge the pleasure of wearing them, you go because you like walking anyway and would go in wellies if they were all you had. Or maybe I was just making too much of a dull day?

Robert Penn's book, *It's All About the Bike*, mystifies me. Okay, it's a wonderful history of the evolution of the machine, but am I cycling in reverence for a bicycle or am I using a bike because I need one in my life? I don't owe anything to cycling if the returns from it aren't worth the effort I put in.

I was beginning to understand why most cycling journeys

are under five miles. They are trips to work. And I could see why most cyclists ride cheap hybrids, bikes that they can sit up and look around themselves on. It's because it's not all about the bike – it's about the rider, the person and that person's needs. And if I didn't need to cycle to Strangford to see Kevin or could have done it in the car and saved time to do some work that day, then maybe that is what I should have done.

The challenge was to accept that cycling is sometimes a joy and sometimes not, a bit like going to the pub in that respect. You can have bad evenings there too. But I began to wonder if the thrill was wearing off me and if cycling was losing its hold on me and even if that wasn't a state more natural to my temperament. After all, I had been content not to cycle for years.

Then a late autumn day arrived with hardly a breeze and an almost-warm sun. And I had things to do, none of them crucial to happiness and comfort let alone continued survival, but still they had to be done. And I'd need the car. And parking had got so expensive in Belfast that there would now be no trouble finding a place to leave it for an hour while I went from one shop and office to another.

But as I passed the bike propped by the hall wall, I felt an itch to take it. With the front door open and the freshness of the day in my face I was filled with an urgency to be out on a country road again, not necessarily belting down a steep hill, and preferably not struggling up one either, but tootling along, with my feet locked to the pedals, my hands gripping the bars and the saddle propped snugly under me, absorbed in the comfort of movement and the challenge of wrestling with the machine that complemented my body and carried it. I knew all about how painful and bloody awkward this whole-body lock-on could be, how nothing else demands all the limbs and attention too. It's not as if you can cycle and spare a hand or foot for anything else, whether squeezing a ball or kicking a can; every bit of you is spoken for. And it might be nothing more than play and distraction but I wanted it. I was thinking, is any of this shopping and office-tripping worth giving up a good ride for?

And it didn't feel to me like it was.

13 Into the West

I get occasional invitations to speak in debates or public meetings and by chance that autumn I got two requests to visit west coast universities, one in Limerick and one in Galway. I decided to bring the bike and take a few days to cycle on the coast and hope that no one minded that I was missing work in Belfast. I was Writer in Residence at Queen's University Belfast and universities are fairly indulgent of writers who disappear from their offices for a few days, so long as they are not actually failing to turn up for classes they are scheduled to teach. I would turn both visits into little tours of places I had ridden through before, many years earlier. I had the bike and I had the legs to drive it with now, and I wasn't going to bother looking at the weather forecast in case it discouraged me. I was going to be back on the road without a plan, letting things happen.

The first time the bike had two panniers on it, it felt well balanced and solid, as if it had assumed the nature for which it was created. When I sat in the station waiting for the train I just felt like admiring the bike, all loaded up, as if it was a statement about me, that I was free and sufficient.

'Are you sure you haven't forgotten anything?' said Maureen when I left the house.

'Of course I have. Don't I always?'

At the station I met another cyclist – Jim, a retired teacher. We wheeled our bikes to the lift down to the platform, queueing with others who were too infirm to take the stairs, and leaned them by each other in the guard's carriage at the front. 'Should we lock them? Are they safe?'

'Don't worry,' said the guard, lounging in a seat in first class. 'Unless this fella here decides to take off.'

His mate smiled as if he thought this was a prospect. But we couldn't sit in first class and keep an eye on them and had to go back through three carriages.

I sat with Jim. He said he was in his seventies now, ten years past a heart attack and feeling fit. 'I go hill walking with a friend every week,' he said. But his friend was away walking in Poland so Jim was taking the bike to Newry, planning to cycle along the Newry Canal to connect with the train again at Portadown. The SmartPass for the over-sixties augments a lot of cycling miles now. 'The strange thing is, I look in the mirror and see an older man but in my head I am about forty,' he said. 'I never expected this.' I said I supposed there were a lot of people of forty who feel older than they should.

When Jim left at Newry I got talking to Hugh who was sitting beside me. He said he was eighty-two and just going to Dublin on his SmartPass to get out of the house. And suddenly from feeling adventurous, like Jim, I saw myself as part of a culture of older men escaping the domestic life. Hugh talked of his wife worrying about him going away for the day. 'She'll do nothing but fret till I get back.' Given that he was blind, she had reason to. The train crunched to a halt short of Dublin and was delayed by an hour but Hugh smiled through all the stress of it, as others muttered and one even pleaded on the phone with his partner to believe that the delay was not his fault. 'You tell her,' he said, and handed me his phone. I took it and said into the silence on the other end, 'Hello. I'm on the train with your friend and we are stuck on the line outside Connolly Station, staring out of the window at Croke Park.'

'It's not just the train,' she said. 'It's everything.'

'Well, in so far as it's partly about the train, that part isn't his fault.'

Eventually we began to nudge forward and the passengers all stood to cluster round the door. A man finishing a glass of beer said to me, 'This is my first time in Dublin.'

'SmartPass?'

'Yes, I just got it.'

I advised the man who handed me his phone to ask for a complaint form. 'You'll get a refund.'

'I think I'll try that,' said SmartPass.

'That would be a good one.'

I had to rush to the front of the train along the platform to get the bike. Then I had to hug it close on the down escalator to the street and set off into the city across the river. This was a part of the journey that bothered Maureen – all these lone travelling men with wives at home worrying about them; that's what comes of giving free travel to old people! But the cycle lane seemed safe enough. I fell in beside another cyclist and asked him if I was going the right way to Heuston station. 'Straight ahead.' I cycled along the full length of my next train, to Limerick, looking for a guard's carriage to stow the bike in but couldn't find one. The driver's window was open so I asked him if he knew where I could put it. He didn't but he'd oblige me by looking. And there it was in the carriage right behind him, a pair of rails for the bike to somehow rest in and straps for tying it up. Unfortunately this system put all the weight on to the mudguard at the back and buckled it, but I thought it would have seemed wimpish to complain.

Getting out of Limerick, next morning, was simple enough though the dual carriageway turned into a motorway and I had to turn off on to narrow country roads. By then the rain was appalling and I had the old problem of not being able to read my map through wet and misted glasses. You just know in a situation like that that you are going to feel no comfort or respite for hours, that you are just going to have to keep plodding over hills in the rain and that at the end of it, if there is an end, you will be soaked and sore.

But the numbing of the senses had other benefits, for when I fell over again for want of being able to detach a cleat in time, my brain and my reflexes dulled by tedium, I didn't feel any pain. I had stopped on a roundabout to try and work out from my maps whether I should go off the motorway to the west and round Shannon, or to the east and into the hills when I slammed into a crash barrier which, impacting a little higher, might have taken some ribs. As it was, I was still so muffled by delirium and suppressed anxiety, as if my brain had pulled a duvet around itself, that I did not even notice the scrape on my left lower arm until it began to sting in the shower that night.

I'd decided to have lunch in Ennis. After chaining up the bike I walked into a hotel. A sign on the door urged patrons to wipe their feet. That should have been a warning. A man who has cycled dozens of miles – well a couple of dozen miles – in heavy rain, does not look like the sort of person you'd like to have in your dining room. I asked the way to the restaurant. A shocked waitress urged me to go into the bar. So I did. I was too hungry to be indignant.

The road to Milltown Malbay is essentially a meandering mountain road across County Clare. It is only for heroic cyclists who are fresh and eager for challenge. It is a devious, insidious and pernicious ribbon of tarmac, in which many of the hills are stepped but each ascent is concealed by a corner that seems to promise a little relief. You don't know until you are round that corner that you have further to climb; your heart has been dallying with the fantasy that your struggle will end there and you'll be able to roll downhill for a couple of miles. You pace yourself to collapse exhausted at the bend ahead then find when you reach it that the gradient, till then concealed from view, gets sharper still.

I dragged myself up those hills and by Connolly, disheartened by the discovery that I could have taken a shorter route on the cycle and walking path, I resolved to take the next B&B I saw. It was in Milltown Malbay, a place I had already accepted in my water that I would not see that day. I hadn't understood that finding a room for the night would would be a long and complicated quest.

The man who answered the first door I called at said he was sure I would have no trouble getting someone to take me, but not in his house. 'We have the decorators in.'

So I wheeled myself into town, buoyed up by his encouragement. At the first crossroad there was a bar/restaurant B&B. I parked the bike outside and went into the hallway. Through a side door from the hall to the bar I saw a slightly dilapidated fat woman on a high stool. She scoffed at me as if she had me sussed. 'Are you an early riser?' I took this not to be a test question but simply a hint that she'd rather I went away. I was beginning to understand that a sign in front of a house declaring it to be a bed-and-breakfast establishment was not always to be construed as a warm invitation to passing travellers. 'Oh I am indeed.'

'In that case, there's no bed here for you.'

I had thought blithely that, this being Ireland of the broken banks, business people would be hungry for custom. Clearly there were complexities that I had not yet taken into account.

I crossed the road to a pub. The landlord stood at the bar chatting to customers who were as relaxed as most people would be in their own homes. He had a room. It was twenty-five euro, bed-and-breakfast. There were three keys I had to acquaint myself with. I went upstairs and looked at the room. There were two single beds there side by side. One had the bedding turned down, suggesting that someone had been sleeping in it. 'Oh yes, I forgot about that,' said the landlord. He thought for a bit then offered me another key. 'Same as the first. Thirty euro. I did mention we don't do breakfast.' I wondered if I was being spurned by Milltown Malbay and directed towards Spanish Point, two miles away, and the nice hotel there. I locked up my bike before going in, confident that I was at the end of my journey. But they wanted ninety euro B&B and I wanted to pay less. And it was now seven o'clock and getting dark.

I saw a house nearby with a large B&B sign in front of it. When I reached it, it turned out to be an advert for another house a kilometre away. I didn't like the sneakiness of this so I turned in the other direction along the shore. There I saw the coastal guesthouse with a sign reading Vacancies. But no one answered the bell. Then I found a note on the glass beside the door with a phone number for prospective sleepers. I called it. It was a hotel further down the road. How much? Forty-five euro. Okay. The last part of the game was to pass a nice B&B and a big swanky hotel restaurant and to wonder if I was meant to choose between them or just go on to the hotel which had answered the phone. I chose to do that. The food was glorious. Chowder with dash of Pernod in it. The room, however, was cramped, drab and functional. It would do. But I had a feeling I had not won first prize.

In the morning I tried to recover my memory of Spanish Point and locate the hostel and the spot where Alanna and I had camped, and I had sung for Christy Moore. The woman in the hotel said there hadn't been a hostel here for years. But I did see the flat ground by the river and the arch of the bridge which had separated us from the campsite, now being rebuilt with men on scaffolding across it. Five donkeys grazed there.

In the breakfast room the anodyne and heartless versions of Irish songs played to the hungover golfers included a plastic remake of 'Bright Blue Rose', a song that Christy had sung that night. The woman at the desk asked if I had been comfortable. 'No,' I said. 'The room was much too small. More like a cabin than a bedroom.'

Once mounted I took my pace gently. From Spanish Point I followed the coast to Lahinch. There were a couple of treacherous hills but I didn't mind now. They stop you getting lazy. The lone traveller, taking off on his own, is presumed to be getting closer to his inner being, thinking things through and resolving some of the conflicts of his makeup. If this venture was part pilgrimage, even penitential, I should have been asking myself where I had gone wrong in life and strayed from wholesome natural living and started to squander my health and wellbeing. Actually I had no time for thinking at all, which was as well since there was no simple answer. Much of my life in the years in which I had slowed down and fattened had been good and productive.

Once on the road there is no preoccupation stronger than the road itself, such that at times the mental change of gear required to stop and eat or find a bed for the night, seems to involve a personality change, a concerted will to break the momentum of cycling. So how is a traveller to ask deep questions of the soul, about the direction of life, the job, family, debts or the book of poems or building project that isn't yet finished? It is inconceivable that you can conscientiously attend to practical problems when climbing a hill, when the need to keep moving is more pressing than any other requirement life makes of you.

Yet, when your mind is on things other than your memories, anything can sneak up on you. All the policed and problematic thoughts simply walk in the back door and leave again, disturbing you less for your not having noticed them come in and allowing you to become gradually more familiar with them. So, in the fixation on forward movement, the mind sifts its worries and dispenses with them.

In Lahinch the water was full of surfers and kayakers. In the car park, the surfers struggled into wetsuits. After Liscannor the hills were steeper and more exasperating than they needed to be as mere challenges to my moral ardour and stamina. At the top of one, a full car park served people coming to marvel at the height of the Cliffs of Moher. I thought that if they hadn't driven up the hill but had sweated over every yard of it as I had, they would know how high up they were and wouldn't need to go to the edge and look down.

At Doolin, I sat on the limestone shore and watched a man play his guitar and sing to the rocks and waves. But maybe he didn't like me watching him or maybe he had only come to practise one chord and was happy he had got it right, as after just a few minutes he got up and walked away. Doolin and Spanish Point now looked like fresh new resorts for tourists. When I was young and there for the first time, I thought I was acquainting myself with ancient places. Now I was old, compared to the other eager visitors, the backpackers and the hikers, and the town had been freshened up, revivified, to look as tidy and new as a theme park. I was dazzled by it when I first came, now I thought I had it sussed. And German men and women were getting off big air-conditioned tour buses outside Gus O'Connor's pub, and walking about, perhaps trying to recapture the memory of earlier times when they had themselves been hitchhikers and campers here, learning to play the tin whistle. Maybe some were here for the first time, having read that this was the heart of the Irish folk music culture and thinking they could absorb a little of that spirit just by getting off a bus for an hour and breathing the air.

On the road out of town I was startled by a couple of girls shrieking at me from the window of a car. I could have fallen off. I suppose the attraction of this kind of mischief is in seeing the cyclist startled out of absorption. The rain was coming down on the Burren and putting a sheen on the limestone. If this had been a clear day I would have been able to see across to the Nine Bens in Connemara. Their outline was faint in the mist.

Coming down one horrific hill at speed I met a woman pedalling cheerfully up from the other direction. She smiled. You can get a sense of meeting people in short flashes when cycling. You only make contact for a moment, but it's long enough to get a sense that you have learnt a little about each other. And then I was back in the game of trying to find a bed for the night. Approaching Fanore I opted to skip the first B&B

I saw in favour of one that might have a bar and restaurant nearby. The second was too tempting. I cycled over the metal tubes of the cattle baffler and on to the gravel. But though I saw the set tables inside, no one answered the doorbell. There were two phone numbers on the sign but there was no answer from either.

At the next one a young man came to the door and said, 'Are you on your own?' I naively thought that my being alone made me less trouble, easier to fit in. An older man came out. 'You see, we are going into Lisdoonvarna for the festival and it wouldn't be worth cancelling just for one.' I had not known that this was the last night of the matchmaking festival or I'd have gone to Lisdoonvarna instead myself and sampled the crack. 'Are you looking for a woman yourself?'

'Och no,' he said. 'I just go in for the music.'

He told me he didn't want to see me stuck and there was a room I could have but there would be no breakfast, though I could have a sandwich in the pub next door; it opened about lunchtime. He showed me an apartment with two bedrooms, a living room and a shower and toilet. 'Well if you can leave me a couple of eggs and a few slices of bread, I can make my own breakfast.'

'You'll want a teabag too.'

It was a lovely apartment in a converted attic space under a dormer window with pine stairs up to it from a large kitchen. 'You put on the heat before you go out to the pub and you'll be roasting when you get back, though if you're a cyclist you will not be the cold type anyway.'

In the local pub that night three women were planning their trip to Lisdoonvarna. 'Are you from Ireland yourself?' said one of them.

It was one of those situations where neither side is sure how much curiosity the other will bear, but I would have been happy to chat. Their big concern was getting to the festival. They asked the barman, 'Is there a bus?'

The barman checked with Paddy who said the bus would

leave the front of the bar at a quarter to eleven. The women were only interested in getting the bus back, and were wondering how to find it at the end of the night. 'Sure you might pull a man and not be coming back this way at all,' I said.

'Oh it's not for that we're going but the music.'

My dinner was pan-fried trout and spuds with a pint of Guinness on the side. After physical exertion it is only sensual pleasure that you want so I had a wee Jameson after that. It still wasn't eight o'clock but I was aglow and ready for bed. I lay in my attic listening to the rain spatter the roof and the wind howl round me.

In the morning my tyres were a little soft but I should have left them alone. I don't like these modern pumps that have no intermediary tube to the valve. They impose too much weight on a little thing that is loose and frail. The rear wheel tyre responded to my care and blandishments with a long low derisory hiss.

At that moment the proprietor came out from the B&B in his bare feet, trousers and vest. He said, 'Did you get a few pints in you last night?'

I said I was in bed by nine listening to the rain on the roof. He said, 'I wasn't in my own bed until five in the morning. The girlies half my age were dancing with me and feeding me drink.'

'So there was misbehavin'?'

'Not at all. Is that a problem you have?'

'A puncture.'

I had not changed the tube on a bicycle wheel in twenty or more years, so this would be a challenge to the memory in my fingers. I did recall from my old Raleigh that the last stage of edging the tyre back on could be sore on the thumbs. This tyre was an easier fit.

And though I had been fretting overnight about my low stamina and the difficulty of the journey so far, my muscles had rested with twelve hours sleep and were now primed for a more concerted effort. They might not have been hardened by experience but I felt they now understood that more was expected of them. I took to the road as a stronger fitter man.

I skirted the shore of northwest Clare, where the landscape, roughly scored and with boulders lying about, looks like the aftermath of a riot among giants. I caught the eye of a fisherman walking back from the water's edge. 'Catch anything?'

'Not really.' Whatever that means in the context.

As I entered Ballyvaughan I noticed two men with an old bicycle. One of the men called out to me, 'A great day for a ride.' So I turned and stopped in front of them, taking them for touring cyclists too. The taller man, Rory – as he'd introduce himself – asked where I was from and admired my gear. He gave his friend a summary. 'This is the best of scientific gear you have here,' he said. He admired my waterproofs and my shoes and then talked about how he had come to this area to live an alternative lifestyle.

I was intrigued by his own bike. The sprung saddle had some kind of woven pink cover. 'The ladies like these. They all love them.' I noticed that his two wheels had very different kinds of tyre, a thick heavily treaded tyre on the back and a narrow racing type at the front. And he had a folded blanket draped over the bar for a little girl who now appeared to be his companion. 'Are you a photographer?' she said. I said I was a writer.

'Ah, there is one of the greatest writers of Ireland living just over there,' he said, 'Fintan O'Toole.'

'I know him,' I said, 'but I don't expect he'd welcome a cold call on a Sunday morning.'

'Well, I once called on Michael Viney,' said Rory. 'And though he didn't seem too pleased at first, I believe he warmed to me.'

The road from Ballyvaughan to Kinvarra was gently undulating, with a smooth surface for most of the way. There was one horrific hill that I had to stop for breath on, twice, but there were also some belters of descents. But by Kinvarra the light rain on my glasses made it difficult for me to see ahead or read the B&B signs I was looking out for.

Again, just finding a bed was a bother. 'We are closed,' said a boy at the first. 'Well you might have put something on your sign up on the road then, to notify people there is no point in coming down here.'

He apologised and rang another house for me. 'It's a cyclist. Yes, he's on his own. No I thought not.'

In town I stopped at another B&B and rang the bell. No answer. I went to another, next door, which had a note on the glass directing me back to the one I had just been to. Maybe if I had been patient I'd have found one in which the bell did get answered and there was actually a proprietor amenable to receiving a solitary customer but by now I was sensing that I had grasped the pattern so I crossed the street to the hotel which took me in for sixty euro and even let me park my bicycle under the stairs.

Kinvarra was almost continental in its beauty. I walked along the shore that evening and saw a Norman tower lit up and reflected on the water, a dozen swans in close formation, and I walked past a bar with a music session on to a little Italian restaurant where I had linguine and clams and a couple of glasses of wine.

When I was out on the road I usually phoned Maureen about three times a day, once from the roadside to reassure her I was safe and enjoying myself, once when I had got the room to describe it to her and assure her that I had eaten, and once at night for a cosy chat before going to sleep. I was also able to check my email on my phone and to occasionally update my Facebook status and check on the comments I had provoked. There was no sense of being cut off from the world in the way I was on earlier trips, where the only news was from the morning paper and a call home would have risked alarming the person at the other end, for you could only be calling from a camping holiday if something had gone horribly wrong.

At the very end of the trip, unhooking our bikes in the carriage in Central Station, I met a man called Robin who had been cycling in Mayo. He had a Dawes Galaxy with a sprung Brooks saddle and when I remarked on how nice a bike it was, he said he always thought that other people's bikes were nicer than his own. We discussed the separate journeys we'd made. He'd had no trouble with B&Bs. He said, 'The man I used to do this with couldn't get permission from his wife this year, so I went on my own.'

On a gorgeous bright day in the middle of November, I drove into Westport, with my bicycle strapped to the back of my car. I had taken the circuitous mountain route and hadn't noticed the other cars, similarly slung with bikes converging on the town. When I parked outside the hotel and walked to the back of the car to check the straps, I took approving nods from passers-by, as if they were glad I had made it.

Another car passed me with a nice sleek white racing bike strapped on, and my only curiosity was about the fact that someone with such an expensive bike used the same cheap carrier that I had. I had a meal in the hotel beside two young women, elegantly dressed, as if for a night in the bars, but they were sharing information on where they had left their bikes for the night. When their meals arrived and both started shovelling unappetising heaps of pasta into themselves, I deduced that they were serious racers. They discussed whether to extend their stay. 'Bob has made a shepherd's pie and he'll be wounded if I don't finish it.' So the concerns of the giants among us are no less domestic and partner-centred than those of our own.

At the B&B, the first thing that the man of the house said to me was, 'You want an early call then?' Wasn't I here for the race?

Next day hundreds of fit young athletes would be taking

on the Sea 2 Summit challenge, entailing a run, cycle race and a climb up the holy mountain of Croagh Patrick. I suddenly felt that I should retrace my steps to explain to all the people who had shared knowing looks with me that I was not the champion of the roads they had taken me for. I could at least correct my landlord's impression that I was someone who had such a command of my body and my bike that I might have the gall to challenge hundreds of people a third of my age.

No, I was here to try out the cycle path between Westport and Mulranny, having read reviews of it in the *Irish Times* and seen photographs of the mountains and the bay on either side. Ethical Traveller in the *Irish Times*, praising the Mayo cycling routes between Achill and Westport (*Irish Times*, 16 July 2011) described the pleasure of riding on an electric bike and recommended the services of bike hire companies which send minibuses to pick you up when you're exhausted and can go no further. This was a tourist attraction for people who are little more than fit enough to just get on to a bike. The cycle track mostly covers an old railway line. It is practically level all the way and is pitched by Mayo tourist authorities as an attraction even for people who hardly cycle at all.

The embarrassment of being taken for a man who is superfit, or at least thinks he is, followed me through the trip. But there was another event in the town which was potentially more suited to me, a book festival. On my first night I went down to the Sea Sky Shore art gallery for a glass of wine at an opening. On show were the works of Fionntan Gogarty and Jimmy Lawlor. Gogarty does strange things with paper he makes himself: he overlays and colours and then writes on it. More intelligibly, he also does beautiful, almost photographically exact paintings of beach pebbles. Lawlor is a sort of surrealist cartoonist. He paints beautiful images representing bad jokes. One has a child drawing a hare on a little trolley and the title is 'Pulling A Fast One'. We'd have got the joke if he had just done a sketch.

I had made the mistake of arriving on time, when there

was hardly anyone else there. I made the same mistake again at the grand opening of the festival an hour later and found myself standing around a virtually empty hall looking like someone who had no friends or any particular idea of how to enjoy himself on a Friday night in Westport. In time, dozens of people trickled in and then the travel writer Manchán Magan stood and gave us an impassioned speech about how we had to reconnect with Ireland, and then there was a two-man show celebrating the work of Bob Dylan.

In my little room in the B&B that night, I heard a couple of young men arrive for the race and get themselves to bed early. They sounded like big fellows, the sort that can't help the noise they make or the space they take up. They would whisper in the hall but could do nothing about footsteps that trundled and scuffed as they moved. Even without seeing them, I guessed they were built for the challenge of the race. They were up and away before me in the morning.

I stood at the door to check the weather. A pesky drizzle hung like contagion in the air, thick and unwavering, in full occupation of the day, as if it owned the whole country. The tarmac shone as if it was pleased with rain as an adornment and the clouds were too heavy and dark to be distinguishable from each other. Nothing I saw offered me hope. I wrestled my way into my rain gear and strapped up my shoes. I decided I had no choice but to cycle today or the trip would be wasted.

The cycle track runs from Westport, through Newport and Mulranny. Newport is now the centre of a tourism drive built around cycling. Governments don't build embankments or cut through hills to smooth the way for people on bikes but they can allow them to use the old earthworks they erected for the train and then discarded. When the racers set off on the greenway south and west, to start their exhausting challenge, I threw a leg over my bike and headed north for a tootle.

My first impression of the greenway was good. The rain suddenly cleared and the sun came out. Astonishing. Suddenly the sky was blue and I was so warm that I had to take off some of my layers. This was the middle of November but I'd be fine. For part of the way a jogger ran in front of me. I began to feel a little indignant at the proof that my cycling was no faster than a man running. This suggested that going on a bike was just cheating. But after a mile I overtook him and gave him a little wave to reassure him I wasn't competing, though I was.

The track runs alongside the main road to Newport, through woodland and by fields of pasture. There are lovely little bridges erected over streams and maps posted too. You would not get lost there. But the track surface began to annoy me. It was black rough tarmac, coated with fine grit. So all the way I could hear the crunching of my tyres on the little chippings and I felt that my wheels had a poor purchase on the surface. Maybe the planners had been thinking of mountain bikers and their love of rugged terrain but to a road tourer like me, this seemed an unnecessary complication. The Comber Greenway in Belfast has smooth tarmac and is much easier to ride on.

I was actually relieved when the track was abruptly broken and I was diverted on to the main road for the last two miles into Newport.

After Newport, the track enters the most beautiful countryside in Ireland along the north coast of Clew Bay, an area garlanded with islands and peaks. But much of the track was shielded from the sea view and the straight level route might have contributed greatly to the comfort of rail travellers but, against a strong desire to enjoy this trip, I started to find it boring and tedious. I wondered how this could possibly have given such pleasure to Ethical Traveller, the *Irish Times* writer who had covered it on an electric bike.

I shouldn't sneer. I should be more considerate of those who would let the bicycle evolve into a lean motorbike. The difference between us is that I seem to relish the pain, the satisfaction of having exerted myself.

The beauty of the bike is that it is purely mechanical and that it is, even so, a sufficient vehicle for a healthy human.

Yet, in the very same edition of the *Irish Times*, there was an article sneering at the e-book as the unnecessary ruination of the printed volume and the multi-sensory experience of reading. That was a theme running through the whole issue, with writers celebrating the pencil sharpener and fountain pen, but taking the opposite view on a bicycle as if it alone, among the artefacts we have loved, still isn't good enough.

Every so often, the view of the bay in the hills around me would open up, including Croagh Patrick in the mist on the other side, where the triathaloners were struggling. I could empathise with them because I had climbed that mountain myself three years earlier, when there was about fifteen per cent more of me to haul up there. It is a beautiful mountain to look at but the last part of the ascent is horrific. There is only unstable scree to put your foot on. I was glad I wasn't up there now.

And I would stop and savour the grandeur and the glory and slug some more water and chew some nuts. I might have been perfectly contented to sit there in a windbreak all day and feel the heat of the sun on my body, knowing that I was in one of the most beautiful places on earth, where just being still one might feel enriched and happy. The last thing a poet would have done to this landscape would have been to carve a level, straight line through it and the most heartless way to respond to it would be to treat it as an outdoor gymnasium.

I plodded all over this minimally varied route taking little pleasure from the physical exertion. I might as well have been on an exercise bike. Yet a lot of people had come here and seemed to be enjoying it. And the fact of there being so many people cycling the Irish countryside in the middle of November spoke of a widespread eagerness to cycle the countryside. Could Mayo not have given them better than this?

One man of about my own age overtook me. He was definitely out training and paying little attention to the sheen of sunlight on the heathered hills. Many of the cyclists I saw were beginners; a girl coming the other way was giggling shrilly at the prospect of bumping into me, when in fact she had plenty of space. Catherine, a woman I talked to in Mulranny, told me that she hadn't cycled in a long time and was having trouble with the gears.

And at this stage, the drabness of the actual cycling had not dimmed my wonder at the views of the mountains and the bay, but about halfway back the balance began to change and my exasperation rose. This wasn't a difficult trip; it just felt unnatural and unchanging, the same thing mile after mile. The only thing wrong with this place was the path.

A group of about twenty pesky little birds scattered out of a bush when they saw me coming and flocked to another bush, further along, to be safe from me, only to be hardly settled before my steady oncoming unnerved them again. And for about a mile they danced in the air in front of me like wind-scattered leaves, always seeming to think that one more hop would take them out of my way but never working out that the predictor of where I would go next was this ugly path which, for some reason, they seemed themselves to want to keep to.

I turned a corner into a group of people talking together, two young cyclists sitting on a wall, the bikes propped opposite them, and two older men I took to be local farmers. 'This is a conference?' I said.

'And where are you from?'

I said I'd come from Belfast, though not just that morning, and wasn't it a marvellous day?

'Now, it's been raining all week.'

One of the men bent over my little mirror and said, 'Begod, a mirror on a bike. I mind the time we didn't even have them on the tractors.'

The first speaker asked me what I thought of the cycle path and I said I didn't like the surface.

'I've heard that said, right enough. Maybe they'll take note and lay smooth tarmac.'

But then maybe walkers, in big boots, like the crunch underfoot.

I looked to the young cyclists sitting on the wall. The girl had proper cycling gear on with a wee skirt over her leggings. She had blonde hair and enormous squarish brown tinted sunglasses. The boy had curly dark hair. 'What do you think of the surface yourselves?'

The boy said, 'Not really having a frame of reference, I couldn't say.'

English. Talking like a student but cycling in November in County Mayo. I didn't think I could ask why. I saw another couple later, the man in an open-necked shirt, smoking as he rode, and behind him a woman in a low-necked dress. They looked no more like natural cyclists than the Pope would have done and had presumably been talked into the idea of trying the Greenway on hired bikes, by their hotel.

Back at the B&B I loaded the bike back on to the car and met the two men who had come for the Sea 2 Summit. They had just showered and changed and were planning to go for a meal or to the pub. One of them was fixing their bikes to the car, waiting for the other, who was just coming down the step when I rolled through the gate and pulled in.

They were tall thin men, perhaps only in their twenties, dressed in jeans and fleecy shirts, looking as well scrubbed and groomed now as their mothers could want them and moving without any hint of fatigue, bruising or strain. I groaned off the bike. I wasn't as weak as I had been after some of my other treks, but I needed to stretch and eat something. I caught sight of my face in the window of my car and I looked bleary and dishevelled. My hair was sticking up. I was sweating and stooped from my efforts and feeling inadequate in the face of their impressive freshness. This might have been the start of the day for them now.

'No, I wasn't in the race,' I said. The danger was that they would take me for a straggler who had only just made it back. Everyone I met would think that if they saw me on the bike or in cycling gear, so I would have to change as quickly as I could back into the normal attire of an ordinary man.

'I just came for a wee tootle on the Greenway. A lovely day for it.'

But they were curious. How far had I gone? One of them was eyeing the bike. He was probably trying to work out the logic of it, heavy but shaped like a racer, yet geared for hills.

'Just to Mulranny. About forty miles.'

'Wow,' he said, turning to his friend, 'I don't think I'd be up to that.'

I could have kissed him.

But that was the last big run of the year as the evenings darkened and the mornings got colder. Then the bike built for distance and heavy loads became simply my vehicle for getting to work on. Most of the cycling bloggers I followed had several bikes for different purposes. I had the one and it wasn't of the type that other commuters were using. The people I passed in the mornings on the Ormeau Road mostly preferred little hybrid machines with smaller wheels and fatter tyres, squat frames and straight handlebars.

The hardy cyclists carry on through the winter. In cold weather you soon warm up on a bike. I'd rather have my fingers free to feel a good grip on the handlebars and the gears. I have reflexes that understand the minute tweaks and these are muffled by my gloves, but they'd be numb anyway without them. The bike itself is cold to the touch but more forgiving on ice than you'd expect, as you'd need it to be. Ice doesn't clear from cycle lanes as quickly as it does from main roads. The cars will have scrubbed the road surfaces more thoroughly than the narrow wheels of the fewer bikes out on a morning can do.

On the first icy morning of the year, the cycle lanes were littered with twigs off the trees from a winter storm. I knew

I would be okay so long as none of this wood was strong enough to topple me or puncture my tyre and I didn't skid. And when I doubted the sense of coming out on a bike, the wheel marks in the frost offered proof that others had made it through even earlier. If they could do it, so could I. As I passed the waste depot a lorry turned in without seeing me, without the driver even looking for me. Cycle lanes aren't really traffic routes to a lot of drivers. Then a man lifted a child out of a parked car at the nursery and set her down on the edge of the cycle lane, taking it for a footpath. She was wrapped up in a purple anorak and a woollen hat. Would she see me, let alone know not to step backwards in front of me? Daddy had no bike-sense either.

Once on to the main road I had half of the footpath, designated for bikes by a thick white line down the middle. The surface tilted towards the road and was slushy. My main danger here was people not seeing me. I wanted a steady pace to warm my bones and skin but I didn't want to have to brake suddenly where a skid might take me into the line of cars coming out of town. The river was a channel for cold air coming off the sea. A merciless breeze seeped in through the gaps in my clothing. The pedestrians were huddled into themselves, worse off than me for not moving vigorously enough to generate the body heat that might protect them.

I followed the river on the north side. First I had to chance the slope that would take me down level with it. My tyres had a better purchase on the ice than any pair of shoes I had ever owned but the damage from a skid here would be worse than a tumble at ground level. Still, pinching the brakes yard by yard would hardly help. I chose to roll and I was fine.

Now I had space to look around and see what a beautiful morning this was. And I was warm already. The air was metallically sharp and bright. The sun was low and cutting shadows precisely. I didn't have a camera with me. Across the river was the park, a luxuriant indulgence of urban space for an experiment in contrasting types of woodland for the magpies and grey squirrels. This morning, only people with needs would be there; mothers wheeling children to nurseries and minders, dog walkers who had to come out whatever the weather.

I had small cramped streets to my left, gable walls and then sports fields, then the railway line. Everywhere people were rousing themselves or shuffling uncomfortably towards their day. Some clung to the railings or to each other over the most slippery patches. Ahead there was a hump bridge and I forced a little speed to take it without having to pant or shift gear on the rise. Whoop and I was over and practically sailing, the river on my right casting golden light that was chopped into flashes by the railings while a train shunted in the other direction on my right and the few passengers at the window seemed unimpressed. They hadn't even taken their coats off.

Another little hillock took me up on to the road again, on the Albert Bridge, where I crossed with the pedestrians then followed the footpath towards the Waterfront Hall. The sign said I should dismount here but I trusted myself to negotiate the dismal, distracted walkers; no point in relying on them to jump out of the way at the sound of the bell. There was a woman in a long black coat that was draped like a blanket. I was wondering how uncomfortable that man with a shaved head must be without a hat. There was a young man in T-shirt and jeans who either couldn't afford clothes or was dressed to impress, like the school girls who walked over ice in shoes as fine as dancing pumps. If they noticed me at all they perhaps wondered what fool or unfortunate had to ride a bicycle to work on a morning like this.

The other cyclists passed with a nod as if sharing a secret. They were as varied as the pedestrians. Many of them were faster than me and some glided past me on racing bikes. These were as impractical in their style for a day like this as the pumps on the girls, no mudguards or carrier, the riders wearing wee rucksacks strapped to their backs. Some were on heavier, squat bikes with broad tyres. And some had old bikes improvised from parts picked up in scrap yards or other people's garages. They were not cycling for pleasure or self-esteem, just getting about as best they could.

The stepped and flagged surface spread around the Waterfront Hall was like a play space for bikers and skateboarders. I was tempted into antics. I might slalom bollards, chance a rear wheel skid. I was at the heart of the fretful city, making good time, enjoying myself. There was a little avenue of arches that might just have been erected for the cyclists and the wiry statue of a woman, holding up a hoop. If she knew the history of this city, a better symbol of life and prospects would be a bicycle wheel, for we all cycled before we drove cars and we cycle again after we give up our cars.

There's the truth of it; I was smug on my bike. No car could have got me through the city as quickly or by a more pleasant route. With much of the pavement ceded to the cyclist I followed the river to the docks and an office block. The little bicycle shed was built in anticipation of four people needing it out of the hundreds who work there. It was where the smokers stood in, out of the rain.

'Awful morning,' said a woman in a white mac stubbing out her cigarette on cobbles with the toe of her glossy shoe. 'I wish I had stayed in bed.'

Epilogue

I have not recovered the level of fitness I had achieved cycling in my thirties. That was clear when I met up with Toby again and we went for lunch and recalled the trips we had taken, the routine of circling Strangford Lough nearly every Saturday afternoon and doing another thirty-five or fifty-mile trip in the middle of the week. He had been off the bike a few years himself and taken up flying helicopters, though he had a mountain bike and his son rode too. The joy of cycling does seem to run through families.

'Do you remember,' said Toby, 'the time we were in Glencolumbcille?'

Was that the time I was with Peter or was it another time?

'And there was one time,' I said, 'we went out by Hillsborough one evening and came back to the house in Dunluce Avenue and John B. was standing at the step and handed us each a glass of home brew which we gulped down like water. Dodgy thing guzzling beer for a thirst.'

'Was that the night we brought the sofa out into the street?'

'Sure we brought the piano out too.'

'What sort of eejits were we?'

But we recalled the routes that had been our favourites, up

the Antrim coast road, round Strangford Lough, short midweek evening runs of only about thirty miles to Hillsborough and back on country roads. We had been fit and not even known we were fit, just in the normal condition of men enjoying their bodies and their bikes and then partying afterwards to undo all the good of it.

We had been like an informal cycling club, stimulated into being by Toby who was a collector of people. There would have been about a dozen of us who all bought bicycles around that time. None of us were in clubs or raced or thought of the bike as a religious symbol – except maybe Toby himself. There was nothing reverential in our appraisal of the materials and parts. We couldn't have talked about bottom brackets without making a smutty joke. And we argued and paired off and split up and reformed in different permutations and eventually drifted apart.

I have been able to recover some of the fitness and energy I had then but I have to work harder to preserve it. Drinking like we did back then would leave me more exhausted than the cycling has.

I know now that I am a lousy cyclist compared to the racers who take to the road in packs. You see them pumping along but don't see that under their sleek shirts they have heart monitors strapped to their chests and little computers on their handlebars receiving signals from their bodies and calculating how many calories they are losing and keeping themselves within parameters you never heard of. I am going to try to be a little better. I have acquired a wristwatch with global positioning built into it. It beeps when I lose contact with the mother-ship. At least it always tells the right time.

I have not been systematic and I should have been; it is what all my cycling friends tell me. And am I on the right bike? Did I measure the degree of trail, calculated from the curvature of the forks that hold the front wheel on? No I didn't. Since I returned to cycling I have discovered a thousand considerations I should have dealt with before buying my bike.

In fact, the plain common sense of it is that I should have three bikes at least, one for commuting, one for training and one for touring. The one I have will do for the touring. I think I have established that already.

But are the tyres right? Some of the reviews of my Panorama say I am mad to keep the tyres that come with it because they are too slow. As for the saddle; there are serious bikers out there who tell you that nothing is as good for your bottom as a Brooks but there are others who say that's old hat. I should buy one and try it out but the standard advice includes the warning that I wouldn't have it broken in until I had done a thousand miles on it. I am not confident that the saddle would give way before my flesh did.

I have also slackened my commitment through the winter. A real cyclist would have been out there beating the roads in the dark. My failing is in that I think the bicycle is for me when I should be living for the bicycle. But I have done enough in the past year to be able to sound like a real cyclist. I have tootled along riverbanks and slogged up mountain roads, and earned my dinner at the end of the day and the plaudits of women. I can pass myself off as the real thing.

I can ride some distance with no hands now. I have a sense of a symbiotic bonding with my bike. I realised I had been lucky in my choice or in the advice I had taken at Bike Dock, for a poor fit would have obliged me to buy another. I'm sure that my riding with no hands looks insufferably cool and that perhaps no man of my age has ever done it before, but the truth of it is that it is wonderfully relaxing; it enables me to sit high and ease the stiffness out of my back. I suspect the purists know that you are not really riding a bicycle properly at all unless you are steering with your hips.

About halfway through the project I set myself, of making a real cyclist out of myself, I reframed my philosophy. I abandoned any notion that my objective should be to get superfit and to chalk up hundreds, even thousands of miles. I conceived the idea of the cyclist as tootler. I wanted to enjoy the whole experience and recover the fun I had as a child on borrowed bikes, to extend into long distance travel, over hills and along river banks, something of the thrill I get weaving through the park with my hands off the bars.

And yet much of my story of the past year does little to advertise cycling as pleasure. At times it was agony.

The fit cyclists in the clubs, who race along the roads on Sunday mornings with their heart monitors would say that much of my cycling is a waste of time. I was hurting myself and, because I was not exercising systematically, I was not getting the benefit of the effort – I could have got trimmer and fitter even with less work if I had understood as well as they do how the body works. And that is probably right.

And if you are my age and a bit tubby like me and, instead of wanting to be a child again or indulge some kind of fantasy life on a bike, you'd like to be sleek and impress women, then do it their way. If you only want to be fit, I have an even better suggestion for you than cycling the roads: get an exercise bike and plant it in front of a television in a spare room in your house. If you can get the miles in without being bored, you'll have conquered not only the flab but the hungers of an active human imagination. You'll be like the yogi who developed exercises that would keep his body supple and allow his bowels to function smoothly without ever leaving his cave.

As for me, I can't bear to think that my cycling should always be productive. There has always been something a little ridiculous, I know, about my urge to suffer out on the road, indulging despair as well as occasional elation.

I had got my bike for the mixed motives of preserving my health and fitness and feeling young again, of reliving a fantasy life on country roads, of testing myself against physical limits and proving myself a man, of having great thrills rolling down mountains on the improbable pivot of a pair of narrow wheels. And I had kept my weight off for a year when other slimmers I knew were already piling theirs back on. And I had been over much of Ireland driven by the only two pistons nature gave me, my own wee legs, sometimes heaving with exasperation, sometimes almost afloat on the breeze.

And what remained strongest at the end of the year was the fun of it and the freedom. I feel I have clawed something back from the demands of life by taking pleasure in simply riding my bike to work. I hope it was the same for my father when he was rolling downhill into Ballycastle to visit his family after hours crossing county Antrim, and that the bike and the breeze took his mind off his onerous duties.

I am now sixty-one years old, which logically should be still worse than being sixty, since the extra year has ticked off more of life. Strangely the passing of the years between the big cusps of decades has never been as unsettling for me. I expect turning seventy to come round faster than it should and to be horribly disheartening, but who knows? I may be a really good cyclist by then, with legs of steel and a paunch as tight as a drum-skin. Or I may have been depleted by something that was not foreseen, as in the little blood test that told me I was too fat to process sugar and should get back on the bike. I could get run over by a bus in the morning. Maybe the fret about how little of life is left comes when we fear that the life we are living is just too short and also not good enough. Not all of one's destiny is manageable through diet and exercise, but the answer to that is that when you are out on your bike, whether slaloming jellyfish on Rossnowlagh beach or puffing past the Cliffs of Moher, you're enjoying yourself in the moment and not thinking about how long it lasts.